Praise for
A Kind of Mirraculas Paradise

"Insightful . . . Allen offers readers an incredible glimpse into the life of a person battling with schizophrenia."

—*Publishers Weekly*

"A glimpse of how schizophrenia looks and feels from the inside."

—*Kirkus Reviews*

"[A] compelling debut . . . Allen is a skillful writer."

—*Library Journal*, starred review

"Compulsively readable . . . A fascinating and important work."

—*Booklist*

"It is an odd thing, paranoia. It's easily lampooned and culturally accessible, but it's seldom experienced or portrayed so elegantly as Allen does here."

—*Paste Magazine*

"An extraordinarily empathic journey into the mind and lived experience of a man who struggled to understand and explain his life . . . I urge you to let Allen introduce you to [their] uncle Bob."

—*Little Village Magazine*

"This book is an act of radical empathy through which the author—and, vicariously, the reader—enters intimately into a life that would otherwise be unintelligible."

—Anne Fadiman, author of
The Spirit Catches You and You Fall Down

"To pay great attention and devote steady care to the perspective of another is, in itself, almost miraculous—especially when the Other has been cast as mad and dangerous. . . . Allen has brought forward [their] uncle's life, rendering in exquisite detail what his experiences as a stigmatized, struggling man allowed him to see. This is a truly original piece of work. I urge you to read it."

—Adrian Nicole LeBlanc, author of *Random Family*

"A book of many strange and often oddly beautiful pieces that together combine into a story that will make you tremble. [*A Kind of Mirraculas Paradise*] is a resurrection of sorts, a profound retrieval of a life from beyond the veil with which so many of us obscure the realities of illness and family, loneliness and intimacy."

—Jeff Sharlet, author of *The Family*

A KIND OF MIRRACULAS PARADISE

A TRUE STORY ABOUT SCHIZOPHRENIA

SANDY ALLEN

SCRIBNER

New York London Toronto Sydney New Delhi

Scribner
An Imprint of Simon & Schuster, Inc.
1230 Avenue of the Americas
New York, NY 10020

First Scribner paperback edition January 2019

SCRIBNER and design are registered trademarks of The Gale Group, Inc.,
used under license by Simon & Schuster, Inc., the publisher of this work.

For information about special discounts for bulk purchases,
please contact Simon & Schuster Special Sales at 1-866-506-1949
or business@simonandschuster.com.

The Simon & Schuster Speakers Bureau can bring authors to your live event.
For more information or to book an event contact the Simon & Schuster Speakers
Bureau at 1-866-248-3049 or visit our website at www.simonspeakers.com.

Manufactured in the United States of America

1   3   5   7   9   10   8   6   4   2

Library of Congress Control Number: 2017034690

ISBN 978-1-5011-3403-6
ISBN 978-1-5011-3404-3 (pbk)
ISBN 978-1-5011-3405-0 (ebook)

For Uncle Bob

CONTENTS

A KIND OF MIRRACULAS PARADISE

Genesis

Late one hot summer night several years ago, I got a call from a number that wasn't in my phone. I had recently moved to the Midwest for graduate school and was at a party in someone's living room. I wouldn't usually answer such a call, but in recent days I'd met and given my number to a lot of people. I found a bedroom and, shutting the door behind me, answered.

"Hey, man. How you doing?" It was my uncle, my mom's older brother Bob.

Though I couldn't tell you when we'd last spoken, I recognized his voice right away. Bob had been a teenager in Berkeley in the sixties, and his voice sounded stuck there. He sprinkled his sentences with "Yeah, man" and "Right on" and "Far out." He laughed a lot—his was a wild, wheezing laugh—and, given that he was a smoker, his laughs would often devolve into a loud hack.

"Hey, Bob," I said. I set my glass on a dresser and flicked on a light. He asked if I had moved yet, and I said yes. Some relative must have told him that and that I was studying writing.

"Hey, *I* wrote a book, man. I wrote the story of my life," he said.

"Is that right?"

He talked for a while. He asked for my new address, and without much thought, I gave it to him. I told him I had to go, though.

"Oh, alright, sorry, man," he said, and repeated several times,

"Thank you, Sandy, thanks, man." It was unclear what he was thanking me for or what I had agreed to do.

"It's totally fine," I said, and hanging up, quickly forgot about the conversation altogether.

I didn't know my uncle well. The most time I'd spent around him had been when I was a kid, in the nineties. I'd grown up just north of San Francisco, in a little enclave of aging hippies on the coast, and most of the rest of my mom's family lived about an hour away, in the East Bay. Bob's house was somewhere else, somewhere I'd never been. Sometimes Bob would be at my grandfather's house when we went for Christmas. In the summer, my grandfather would fly us all out to his vacation place in northern Minnesota, and sometimes Bob would be there, too.

The property had a main lodge in its center, and an old tennis court, and a dock. Little sandy paths ran through the birches, connecting everything together. The single-family cabins were each named after a different tree. When my parents, my little brother, and I joined, we stayed in a cabin with a sign beside its screen door that read PINE.

Bob was single and didn't have kids. He didn't often water-ski or swim or play tennis. He'd mostly sit off to the side, in the shade, wearing long sleeves and jeans, sometimes a vest. His hair was long and blond beneath a dusty cap, and he wore glasses. He smoked all the time—mostly cigarettes, but sometimes a pipe that smelled like wood and cherries. He didn't sleep in a cabin like the rest of us, but in the lodge, up a dark staircase I don't remember ever ascending.

Bob was a musician, and he knew I liked to sing. In the evenings, before the bell in the lodge was rung for dinner, I'd hear him playing guitar through our cabin's screen. I'd go sit beside him. I'd fiddle with the moss on the cement step and Bob would strum, and we'd try to figure out what to play. We didn't know many of the same songs. Sometimes we just took turns describing those we did know. Sometimes he just played, or I just sang. Sometimes we made up songs together, songs that were absurd and funny to either or both of us. If you'd asked me then, that would have been my main opinion of my uncle Bob: he was hilarious.

One day Bob and I were buckled into the backseat of a rental car, waiting for someone to drive us into the town nearby, probably to play miniature golf and get ice cream. From his pocket, Bob pulled out a powdery plastic bag of pills. He removed one, held it up, and then chewed it with his teeth, like steak. He laughed like he wanted me to laugh, too. So I did.

He produced another pill and did the same. Several pills later, the ritual was finished and he put the bag away. Something was frightening about this.

"Why are you taking pills?" I asked.

"It's noon. Gotta take pills at noon," he said, and grinned.

I smiled back.

Later I found my mom. She spent her days down on the dock, wearing sunglasses and a big hat, killing mosquitoes and horse-flies with a pair of swatters.

"Why does Bob take pills at noon?" I asked.

The lake's water stank in the midsummer heat.

"Because he's crazy," she answered.

"Why?"

"I think Dad sent him to military schools after the divorce or something," she said, "and he got messed up in there."

My mom is a shy woman, and this was the kind of topic that made her face redden and her voice fall.

He'd call us fairly often back then.

"Hi, Bobby," my mom would sigh when she'd realize it was him. She'd pace around with the phone to her ear, muttering "Uh-huh" or "Yeah," too polite to hang up but also not that interested. Eventually, she'd say she had to go, that she was busy, which was never a lie.

Sometimes she'd hand me the phone. He'd say, "Hey, Sandy,"

and launch right into talking about whatever was going on where he lived—a neighbor who kept bees, a friend who was going panning for gold. He'd talk about stuff he'd seen on TV. He'd ask me questions about my interests and schoolwork, and no matter what I said, he'd seem really interested, saying, "That right, man?" and "Far out."

He'd mail us cassettes of his music, which were labeled things like "HERMIT" and "March 96." His songs were long, sometimes very long, and unvaried, always low and melancholy. Sometimes there'd be a noodling electric guitar, or a synthesized drumbeat, or unintelligible vocals, like someone yelling underwater. Sometimes he'd share a new song by playing it into our answering machine. Occasionally, he ran out our tape.

He'd leave comedic monologues on our answering machine, too, ones performed as a duo of characters he'd created by recording his voice and then either speeding it up or slowing it down. The first character was called the Slow Man. His messages always began "Helllllllo. This. Is. The. Sloooooow. Maaaan." The fast-talking character was called Timothy Headache. Timothy Headache usually wanted something—to sell you a car or be elected to office. His messages would screech real fast: "Hey oh boy this is Timothy Headache and wow have I got a deal for you!" In fourth grade, I'd perform imitations of both the Slow Man and Timothy Headache to my friends at recess. I referred to their creator as "my crazy uncle Bob."

What "crazy" meant I wasn't exactly sure, and the fact that I didn't understand it bothered me. As a child, I often quizzed the adults I knew about their pasts, and back then I'd ask my mom fairly often about her brother, about what happened to him and why. About why their parents had divorced, and why Bob lived with just their father after the divorce while my mom and her sister lived with their mother. My mom didn't seem to know the answers to these questions. She didn't like talking about her past, often saying she had a bad memory. My mom, whose family called her Debbie, had been the baby of her family, four and five years younger than Bob and their older sister, respectively. My mom was quiet, like her dad. My sense was that, as her family split apart over the course of the sixties, few in her family paid her much mind. I picture her, little pretty Debbie with her milky hair, running by and out of view.

Her explanation about her brother—something about a military school—remained unsatisfying. She remembered going to see him in the hospital. It was "creepy," she said. Guys in pajamas, smoking cigarettes, strung out. When I was a little older, she admitted that whatever had happened to Bob may have had to do with drugs.

At some point, Bob stopped joining us on those vacations to Minnesota. I don't know that I noticed his absence all that much; we stopped going, too, when I was in middle school. Eventually, he stopped driving down for Christmas, though again I didn't much notice, and at some point his calls mostly stopped, maybe because we got better at not answering. On holidays, though, Thanksgiving, or one of our birthdays, he'd call in the morning. First thing the phone would ring, and my mom would say, "That's Bobby."

The idea of going to visit Bob never came up during my childhood. A few times a year we'd drive to the East Bay to see my mom's other relatives. For a long time I figured he must have just lived too far away. Later, I realized this wasn't true; his house was only about three hours north, near the Oregon border.

Once when I was about sixteen, my mom and I even passed near where he lived and we didn't stop to see him. I felt bad, and a few years later, when another opportunity came up to drop by, I decided I would. I was road-tripping with a couple friends across the country in their two cars, which they wanted back at school, and realized our route would take us right near Bob's house. I dug up his number and asked if it'd be alright if some friends and I stopped by to see him the next day.

He sounded so shocked and thrilled.

As we sped up I-5 the next morning, I contemplated this decision I had made to go see my uncle. I had no idea what his house would be like or what state it'd be in. I couldn't remember when I'd last seen him. I apologized to my friends in advance for whatever happened. We could stop at Wendy's or something after, I said. I'd buy them lunch.

Off his exit were mostly parking lots. Plastic trash wafted on chain-link fences. We continued out into the country, where the hard red earth was dotted with occasional houses and oak trees. Finally, off a long unpaved road, I spotted his five-digit address.

His home was modest and painted brown and not as ramshackle as I might have guessed it would be. It was August, and so hot our tires swelled.

We parked in front. Bob walked out, as did his two dogs, both girls. They circled us, curious and shy. I had failed to mention that we'd be arriving in two cars; this fact really caught him off guard.

"Driving up here, I thought you were the CIA, man!" he exclaimed several times. I explained what was going on, and he got it and laughed, shaking each of their hands. He was rounder than I had remembered. We hugged briefly, and as we separated, I was startled by how much his face looked like my mom's.

We followed him into his space. It was dark inside—the blinds were drawn—and it stank. It stank like someone had sat inside smoking cigarettes for twenty-five years. The walls were as yellow as his teeth. A television was talking loudly to itself.

My friends and I sat in a row across his peeling faux-leather sofa. Bob lowered himself into a big chair. I realized his bed was also in the living room, right behind his chair. In one motion, he lit a cigarette and looked at each of us, seemingly overjoyed we had come.

He started showing us things. "This is a new television." He tapped its top. "I had the old one on for about twenty years, and it finally died. Don't worry, I got this new one within the hour." He laughed and we all laughed and he coughed.

He next wanted to play us a song, a track he'd recorded. It was like the ones he used to send us—low and slow, with guitar and drum machine and words I couldn't understand. We sat listening and he stared at us.

One of my friends was also a musician and thought Bob might want to hear a song he had recently recorded himself. He took out his iPod and plugged it into the stereo while Bob muttered that he'd never seen such a thing. Bob looked impatient while my friend's song played. In a corner of the ceiling, hanging on a fishing line, was a model of Han Solo's *Millennium Falcon*. The cobwebs clinging to it were thick and orange as coral.

My friend realized that Bob might at least like his new tattoo, given that he liked rock music. It was John Lennon's self-portrait from the cover of *Imagine,* he explained, rolling up his sleeve.

Bob leaped back in horror. "Whoa, man, don't show me that thing!" he yelled. "The government tracks us with those things!" He pointed at me. "Never get one of those, you promise me, Sandra?"

"Okay," I said.

Next he wanted to show us his recording studio. As we followed him down the short hallway, he pointed out a framed poster hanging in his bathroom, a wolf on a cliff beneath an oversize moon. "Isn't that something, man?" he asked me.

His toilet bowl was stained a dark brown.

"Yeah," I said.

The studio occupied what appeared to be the house's bedroom. It was filled with guitars and amps and keyboards and other equipment, all coated with a thick layer of dust. He pointed to a certificate tacked on the wall, something about welding. It had never occurred to me that Bob might have had a job. He pointed to another piece of paper in a frame, something about the military.

"I'm a veteran," he said, which didn't sound to me like it could possibly be true.

He began turning on all his equipment, and as he did, the

anticipatory buzzing in the room grew and grew—everything was already turned up as loud as it could go. He looked at us and grinned, and when he depressed a single key, the whole place quaked as if we were in the belly of a great laughing beast.

Afterward, we sat on his back porch. It was hot enough to make you sick. He served us shrimp that had been arranged on a black plastic tray by someone at a supermarket, and a box of Wheat Thins. I felt terrible that he'd gone out of his way to buy us these things, and I thanked him.

We looked out at his property, the dirt, the wisps of blond grass, the coyote bushes and oak trees. We complimented it, and Bob told us about his neighbors and his irrigation lines in front, which fed a couple saplings.

After a while, my friends walked with Bob back toward the cars. I lagged behind. As I came down the small step off the porch, I felt the wood break beneath me and, stopping myself from falling, turned back to see the stair dangling like a child's tooth.

I could hear Bob and my friends talking on the other side of the house.

I hastened to join them, deciding not to tell Bob what had happened. It was clear the step had been bound to break, and it seemed he didn't often go outside anyway. We had to get going, I told myself, and I didn't want to get into a whole thing with my uncle.

Bob and I hugged goodbye. My friend took a picture of us standing side by side. My friends and I got into our cars. Bob and his dogs returned inside his house. We drove back out of town and away. Countless times since, I've thought about how content I would have been to remain knowing only that much about Bob.

When the fat manila envelope arrived, I wondered for a second what it was.

And then I remembered his call the week before, when he'd asked to mail me something.

Bob had written my new address in Iowa City in large capital letters. He'd affixed a small sticker with his own address in a corner.

Inside was a stack of yellowed paper about a half inch thick. On a piece of notepad paper he'd written a brief note in capital letters: "ITS A HORRIBLE MESS (SPELLING ETC.) BUT I WILL PAY YOU FOR IT PLEASE DONT WORRY ABOUT MY BELIEFS LOVE YA."

I thought back to our conversation, wondering what it was Bob believed he was paying me to do.

I flipped through the pages, which were still curled with the memory of his typewriter and stank like cigarettes. He'd used almost exclusively capital letters, with no paragraph breaks; each page was a wall of text. There were colons everywhere, sometimes big rows of them, and the spelling indeed looked pretty bad. There were places where he'd typed letters on top of one another, or crossed things out and written other things in.

From what I could tell, it seemed to be a rather straightforward autobiography, the facts of his life set down in order. It opened with a description of his life as it was when he was a kid. He stated his father's name and profession. He gave the names and ages of his two sisters. He wrote that he had attended John Muir Elementary School in Berkeley, California, which was

```
VERY DISAPLINED AND FOR THREE YEARS I HAD
A HUGE CRUSH ON A GIRL WHO ALWAYS ENDED
UP IN THE AJACENT CLASS ROOM NEXT TO OURS:
LYDIA TREEANTOPOLIS: I WAS TO SHY TO TELL
HER I LOVED HER.
```

He gave the first and last names of his friends and talked about how they'd spent their time together. It went on:

I WAS ALWAYS THINKING HOW TO IMPRESS LYDIA
BUT SHE WAS HARD TO FIND: I REMEMBER ONCE
IN FOURTH GRADE I WAS REALLY FEELING GOOD
ABOUT MYSELF WHEN MY DAD FIGURED IT WAS
TIME TO GET A CREW CUT: SO HE TOOK ME DOWN
TO THE BARBER, SHAVED MY HEAD AND HAD THE
GUY SHAVE RECEDING BALD SPOTS ON MY FORHEAD
SO I WOULD LOOK LIKE MY DAD: I WAS IN TEARS
BUT THE BARBER AND MY DAD: I HATED THE GUY:
AND TO MAKE THINGS WORSE WHEN I GOT HOME
AND DIDNT WANT ANYONE TO SEE ME, MY SISTER
DEBBIE SAID LYDIA IS OUT IN FRONT OF THE
HOUSE:, MY FIRST CHANCE TO TALK TO HER BUT I
LOOKED LIKE AN IDIOT AND WAS WORRIED ABOUT
SCHOOL THE NEXT DAY ANYWAY: WHAT A BUMBER:

I paused, having read this tale about my grandfather and the haircut. I wondered whether he'd really done that—made a barber shave his son's head so he'd look silly and then laughed at him. I wondered, too, about this girl Bob so loved who'd happened to show up precisely at this humiliating moment.

Perhaps the story was a delusion.

Perhaps it was a lie.

Or perhaps Bob had some kind of agenda. For example, I imagined, perhaps he was upset with his dad and had therefore written this unflattering story to get revenge. (If that was the case, I didn't at all like that he was trying to get me involved.)

Not that I knew much about Bob's relationship with his dad.

I figured Bob relied on my grandfather and his second wife, my step grandmother, Agnes, financially—many in my mom's family did, to some extent. I recalled hearing that they owned the house where Bob lived.

I read a few more pages of the manuscript, to where he described Lake L'Homme Dieu in Minnesota, where he had spent his summers growing up. I'd heard lots about Lake L'Homme Dieu. People on that side of the family—my mother's mother's side— loved to talk about L'Homme Dieu. Whenever they got together, they'd end up telling stories about those good times back then. They'd laugh and laugh until they wiped tears from their eyes. (L'Homme Dieu roughly translates as "man of God" in French, but nobody pronounced it right; they all said "La Hamma Doo.")

I read a few pages further, to where he wrote about being a white student at a newly integrating junior high. I frowned at his descriptions of his black peers. A few pages further and he was at Berkeley High. A slur cut across the page like razor wire. I'd had no idea that Bob, or anyone in my family, was so explicitly racist.

I let myself stop reading.

The manuscript stared back at me.

It was hideous to look at, even from a distance.

Its pages literally reeked.

I wanted to ignore it. I wanted to ignore it the way you ignore a urine-soaked pile of coats on a sidewalk or a man on a park bench screaming obscenities.

I slid the papers back into their sheath and set the envelope into a seldom-opened drawer.

I told myself I was busy, which wasn't a lie.

When he called soon after, I didn't answer. He left a message, asking if I'd read his book. I didn't call back. I felt bad but didn't know what to say. Even if I'd wanted to, and then I did not, I couldn't have simply corrected his spelling and added paragraph breaks and replaced the colons with periods and commas and sent Bob's story off to the presses.

The little of his manuscript that I'd read was partly comprehensible to me, but I had the advantage of being familiar with many of the places and people about which he'd written. Not to mention that I was somewhat accustomed to Bob, to the way he used language, and to his sense of humor.

He left other messages that fall. If he was mad at me for not responding, or hurt, he didn't let on. He always seemed in good spirits, like he was stoked to have just tried me.

I did tell my mom that her brother had sent me something he'd written. She said that sounded "creepy" and that I could throw it out.

I probably would have, but what he'd sent appeared to be an original.

I imagined it had taken him a long time, maybe a really long time, to type it. And given that he called himself a hermit, it seemed unlikely he'd gone to a copy shop and made duplicates. Besides, if he'd done that, wouldn't he have sent me the photocopy and kept the original?

So I held on to it and tried unsuccessfully to forget it was there.

A couple times I randomly decided to show it to friends. I removed it from its envelope and said, "Check this out." They marveled or gawked and tenaciously looked at a page or two. They asked why he sent it to me. "Are you close?" they wondered.

"Not at all," I said. I explained my guess, which was that he wanted help with his writing and I happened to be the only writer he knew.

Sometimes when I passed the drawer, I'd feel a faint curiosity, like a whiff of cherry smoke lingering on a forest trail.

One day a large box arrived for me in my apartment building's lobby.

I lugged it upstairs.

Inside were assorted jams and jellies in little glass jars. It seemed he'd ordered them, maybe from a catalog or QVC. I could not recall Bob ever giving me a gift. I doubted he had much money. I had already felt bad about not reading all of what he'd mailed me, and now I was overcome.

I opened the drawer and set the envelope on my kitchen table.

The least I could do, I told myself, was give his manuscript one good read.

I prepared tea and toast with boysenberry preserves, and I read, for the first time, the whole story of my uncle's life.

I tried to, anyway.

One way to think of what's happened since is I have never stopped reading it.

Not long after I read Bob's manuscript that first time, I was back home in the Bay Area. He again called and this time I answered. I happened to be walking through his hometown, actually, right near UC Berkeley, on my way to plug a meter. I told him so, and he cracked up. Then he got right to it: "Did you read my book?"

"Yeah," I said.

"I don't know many people who've had a life like that."

"I don't know," I said, trying to choose my words carefully.

"Pretty crazy, hey," he said.

"Yeah."

There was a lot then that I didn't know how to feel about the story Bob had sent me and his apparent wish that I help him figure out how to get other people to read it.

I knew there was a lot in those pages that gave me great pause. There was the overt racism, and his other bigoted views—anti-Semitism, homophobia, crude words about kids with disabilities he'd known in a halfway home and also sometimes himself. Many of his descriptions of women did not thrill me.

Mostly, I worried about how candidly he'd written about himself, sharing details about his mental health history, his illegal drug use, and his sexual relationships, including one with a sixteen-year-old when he was twenty-three and working at a gas station. He'd included what seemed like very honest opinions about many controversial topics. He'd written openly about many of our relatives, saying things I assumed they would find upsetting. I worried that he didn't understand the implications of baring himself—and those around us—so honestly to the world.

I was also aware that it certainly didn't seem like Bob had asked anyone's permission to include them in his story. It seemed likely that other people would remember things very differently than he had. I worried that if I helped him, I would jeopardize my relationships with many of the people in question. In some cases, he'd spilled secrets that weren't his to share, some details so private it seemed that repeating them would devastate people I loved.

I had no idea how to say any of this to him, though, that day on the phone.

He was repeating stories from the manuscript, one about a song he'd played on a keyboard and a guitar that had been stolen and a seashell collection that had ended up in a San Francisco museum. I looked at the water and across the bay to the Golden Gate, where the sun was falling fast toward the Pacific.

I finally asked whether he really thought pursuing this project any further was a good idea. "Because," I said, "there are things in there you wouldn't want everyone on earth seeing."

He agreed. He said he wanted two things. First, he wanted his story "out there" because it was "true." But, he added, "I just don't want to hurt my dad."

Sometime after that, I began trying to write an essay about the manuscript Bob had mailed me—and how it contrasted with my memories of him. In that essay, I included both my own sentences as well as lines from his account. The closer I'd read his writing, the more I'd understood it, which makes sense. What surprised me was how much I liked it—his word choices and style. I was loath to do anything but let him speak for himself. So my essay, which I submitted for peer critique, was a sort of patchwork: some of me, then some of Bob in all-capital blocks, spellings and colons and all.

None of my classmates who read that essay liked it, but nobody disliked it for the same reason. Many felt my choice to quote him faithfully was somehow problematic, perhaps condescending. Some found his writing hard to understand. Mostly I observed that few had actually read anything that Bob had written, and I'd included what I'd felt were some of his most powerful sequences. My readers seemed so thrown by the look of his words that they were unwilling to engage with his ideas. It was a feeling I understood, to some extent; my first reaction to his writing had also been to ignore it.

One time I was messing around and I tried writing Bob's story a different way. I had a very strong vision of him getting a knock on his bedroom door and being told to pack his bag. I wrote my version of it, referencing his account as my guide. I kept going, really studying a chunk of his story and then writing it in a way that captured its spirit as vividly as I could.

Writing this way forced me to read his book closely, to try to understand every single phrase, no matter how seemingly unintelligible. Occasionally, I'd still decide that the way he'd put something was just too beautiful or funny or moving—or profane—to change, and so I'd leave it his way. The capitalized words and phrases served as reminders, too, that this was someone else's story.

I've never known what to call my version. Sometimes I call it a "translation," but that's an imperfect term. Sometimes I call it a "cover," as in music. A good cover, I think, may affect a style, but its goal, ultimately, is to convey and affirm the power of the original. For the sake of this exercise, I assumed that all the assertions he made in his manuscript were true, and I confined myself to portraying only what he'd written there.

Many people have asked me why I did this. Why did I choose to write about Bob? What interested me so much about his story? I've never had good answers to these questions. Bob, in his manuscript, described long days out on Lake L'Homme Dieu in the summers fishing. Perhaps it's as simple as Bob was a talented fisherman and I'm the guppy he caught on his line.

Occasionally, I'd let people read what I was writing, and they'd express dissatisfaction with it. Many were curious about lots of things that Bob hadn't included in his manuscript, for example, facts about medicine. Lots of readers wondered whether other people remembered events the same way he did.

I'd argue that I wasn't interested in what anyone else had to say, just what Bob had to say.

Eventually, though, I relented, and began writing this project's second element, the beginning of which you are currently reading.

In many ways, I'm not the best person to have taken on this task; if nothing else, these years have taught me just how true that is.

I haven't lived my uncle's life, and there are ways in which our lived experiences and beliefs differ greatly. I am no expert in so many of the complicated topics at hand. As my grandfather once pointed out to me, incredulously, I think, I was born decades after most of the story occurred.

I have tried to compensate for these deficits. I have tried to learn all I can. I have talked to everyone who'd have me. In some cases, I have changed or omitted names and details. I have made decisions, however wise, about what information belongs.

My shelf of books that relate to this project is now taller than me. Many of the topics it spurred me to research were, I discovered, thorny brambles. Often one book on my shelf would begin shouting at another.

A lot of the fights were about words, about what to call things. As a result, I've thought about how certain words may hold outsize power. How certain words walk around concealing knives that only some people can feel. I have weighed whether to include some particular words in my own version of Bob's story, and have ultimately decided to make my portrait an honest one. Through these years, I've thought a lot about power, too, because that's what these fights often seemed to actually be about.

The fights were also frequently about facts—facts about science, facts about history. The facts I've ultimately chosen to include are here because I think they help situate my uncle's story. I include them despite the fact that, although they may seem stable now, with time these facts might prove radioactive, fall apart, and contaminate their surroundings. My hope is that however I've erred—and it seems inevitable that I have—I have not distracted too much from the task at hand, which is to tell Bob's story as he told it to me.

The more interesting question, I think, isn't why I began writing about my uncle but why I kept going. That I can answer. My initial curiosity about Bob's text was, if anything, artistic; I was a nonfiction writing student. When I told people about my uncle's manuscript, I noticed some seemed to assume that a person like him would be unable to write about himself in a way that counted as nonfiction, which struck me as something worth investigating. Over time, though, because of reading Bob's manuscript so closely, and then because of everything it prompted me to better understand, my motivations shifted. I came to agree with him that we should try to get his story out there.

I read once that every time you access a memory, you alter it, that the synapses themselves are changed. Our most accurate memories are theoretically the ones we most seldom recall. And, conversely, the memories we access most are the least reliable, soiled by the footsteps of recollection. I have often contemplated the irony that, were it not for my uncle having mailed me his manuscript, I never would have thought about him as much as I have. I never would have returned so many times to memories of him from when I was a kid at the lake.

The lodge at dinnertime would be bright and cacophonous— card games paused on tables, babies screaming, dogs running underfoot. Sometimes my grandfather paid to fly out Bob's dog, so she'd be there too. She was small and brown and always trembled. Her name was Shivers.

After dishes had begun and the older adults had returned

to bridge, Bob would go sit on the porch overlooking the lake. He'd light a pipe and strum his guitar.

As the sun descended and the muggy day finally broke, the loons would begin to call to one another. First, you'd hear one long low note from out on the water. Then, from another direction, a reply. Soon several loons would join the chorus, their sound at once beautiful and alien and sad.

Often when I think of Bob, I think of him that way: sitting, smoking, strumming, and singing along with the loons.

IM ROBERT

Bob's first love was a girl called LYDIA TREEANTOPOLIS. They met in third grade. He loved her even though she wasn't in his class; she was always in the other one next door. He'd see her sometimes on the playground and wonder how he might ever impress her.

He had a lot of friends back then, friends whose first and last names he'd remember long into his life. He was always goofing around in class, trying to make them laugh. All the time he'd wind up being made to stay after school, chalk in hand, scratching "I will not talk in class" five hundred times on the vast blackboard.

He and his friends were all traffic boys, which meant they got to direct cars before and after school. Once a year the traffic boys would also perform at a CRAZY DAY FAIR. They'd do a drill on the command of "Simon Says," and if you messed up, you had to sit down.

Once it got to just Bob and his friend Danny, the lieutenant. Danny won, but as Bob jogged back to his seat, he glanced out at the crowd and looked for her.

He wondered if she was out there.

He wondered if she saw him.

By the time he was in sixth grade, his final year at John Muir Elementary, he was a sergeant in the traffic boys. When you were a sergeant, you got to have a whistle. He carried it around all the time, but he was supposed to blow it only before school and after. Bob would place the whistle to his lips, feel its weight and its cool, and blow. Then his troops would help the children safely cross.

Only once had he gotten a good opportunity to talk to her. It was on the same day, back in fourth grade, when his dad had taken him to the barber because he FIGURED IT WAS TIME TO GET A CREW CUT:

The barber hoisted a smock over Bob's little frame. The scissors sneered. His dad looked up from his paper. He was an important man, a professor nearby at the university. He was the one who told the barber what to do next.

The barber plugged his shaver into the wall. Bob felt it trace the back of his neck and then the top of his head.

"Now you'll look just like your dad!" the barber said, his cigarette quaking.

Ash on the floor, and his hair, so blond it was practically white. Tears were falling, too, down Bob's cheeks.

In the car, Bob rubbed the velvet of his newly buzzed hair and felt with horror the two wide tracks of bare skin that now rose from his forehead on either side, meant to make him look like he was balding. Their car ascended the dark and twisty streets.

Bob lived with his dad and mom and two sisters—one older, named Heather, one younger, named Debbie—in an adobe house in the Berkeley Hills. He had his own room that looked over the stoop. Most of the other rooms in the house looked out over the entire Bay Area.

That evening, Debbie said there was someone at the door for him, a girl.

Bob ran to his window, and when he saw her, his insides did somersaults.

Lydia Treeantopolis.

Why had she come to see him?

How had she known where he lived?

He touched his scalp with a shudder.

"I'm not here," he said to Debbie. "Tell her I'm not here."

He watched his sister reappear at the door and say something to Lydia.

Lydia turned and walked up the steps to the street and away.

His crush on her would remain for years, but again, again, she wasn't in his class. Eventually, he never saw her at all. He wondered if she had moved. He would never know why she was at his house that evening. He'd never know how everything would have been different had he gone to the door in spite of his pride. The next day at school, kids laughed at him, and his friend Duncan gave him knuckle rubs on his raw head.

Bob was twelve when the change came. There'd been only one black girl at his elementary school. The most time he'd spent around black kids had been during an intramural football game in sixth grade. He recalled beforehand wondering what these new kids would be like, wondered whether he'd make new friends. It turned out they were IMMENSE IN SIZE and DEADLY SERIOSE IN EXPRESSION. The game itself was a mess—kids tying their flags to their pants so you couldn't yank them off. At one point Bob's team's quarterback got swung around in circles like he was in a cartoon.

Bob stepped off the bus the first day at Willard Junior High and watched the handful of kids from his neighborhood disperse like seagull feathers across a blacktop.

They were shuttled into an unfamiliar gymnasium for a placement test. Bob had never seen so many black people in his life. There were folding tables set up, and booklets, each with a pencil on top. Shouts and screeching chairs echoed through the high ceiling. Bob found his friend Duncan, and together they sat at a table with another girl from their neighborhood, Sarah, who got good grades.

Then something hit him in the back.

Bob whipped around and saw some black kid he didn't know, grinning at him. The kid had hit him!

"What's your problem?" Bob asked.

The kid just kept smiling and walked away.

Duncan said they should go punch him back, and together they rose, but at that moment the principal, who was black and far away on a stage, was telling them to be seated.

Bob saw the kid wave goodbye.

Bob sat. His head churned, and a droplet of sweat splatted on his booklet.

Why had that kid hit him?

What had Bob ever done to him?

He was too riled up to concentrate. He leaned to his left and tried to copy Sarah's answers.

This seemed to be going fine for a while. It wasn't until she finished and he had one question left to answer that he realized he'd been off by one the whole time. In other words, he had every single answer wrong. Sarah rose and walked her test up to the front.

He followed, not knowing what choice he had.

That's how he wound up being the DUMBEST WHITE KID AT WILLARD JUNIOR HIGH. His classes were shit, and he was practically the only kid from his neighborhood in them. All they ever taught about was Africa, Africa, slavery, slavery, and why everything was the white man's fault.

One time a teacher passed out a pamphlet on what sex felt like, and two prostitutes came to their class. Another time an EX CON who'd just gotten out of prison. Such visitors liked to make an example of Bob because he was the only white person around. The EX CON had asked Bob's class, "You ready?"

And Bob, confused as to what the guy was talking about, wondered aloud, "Ready for what?"

THE GUY JUST SMUCKERED, POINTED AT ME AND REPLIED:::YOU AINT READY:::

Everybody burst out laughing—his teacher, the visitor, all the other kids. One kid threw gum in his hair. After class, Bob stood, hands in pockets, as the teacher helped to cut it out.

It was no wonder he got terrible grades.

The only class he didn't suck at was gym.

In gym, in fact, he was excellent, so much so that he got an A+++. The teacher liked to use him as a good example. One time he had Bob face off with this Herculean black kid in front of the whole class. First they had to wrestle; Bob pinned the guy in about four seconds. Then they had to race, climbing up and down the ropes.

He could hear his classmates cheering far below. The whistle blew and Bob sprang, putting fist after fist. At the top, he and his opponent locked eyes. Bob practically slid back down, the rope scorching his palms. The two of them landed with a thud. It was a tie.

This won him a little respect. He got a reputation as a gymnast, one who'd fight back. But kids would still pick on him, and he'd get into fights. Not that this was all that unusual; everybody was always fighting. One white kid was even paying black kids to beat up others he didn't like.

At home, things were hardly better. Ever since the summer after sixth grade, his parents had been fighting all the time too. His dad was always working, but when he was home, they'd be bickering or screaming. Nights filled with their voices.

Then his dad bought a condo nearby—for work— and his mom went BIZERK, accusing his dad of carrying on affairs, and she filed for divorce. OUR WHOLE FAMILY WAS IN HELL, AND SCHOOL SUCKED, AND THERE WAS NOONE TO TELL.

The judge made her put a little telephone in the hallway upstairs, and only their dad had the number; the idea was he could call it to talk to the kids. His mom hated that phone. When it rang and Bob answered, she'd scream at him and he'd scream back. Finally, one night he just ran out the front door. He got on his bike and labored farther up the hill to his dad's new condo. His dad gave him the bed and slept on the sofa.

Later Bob had to go to court and talk to a judge, and then he didn't live with his mom at all anymore, just his dad. His dad got another condo with more room for the two of them.

One night soon after, Bob tried to leave to bike down to his friend Doreen's. They used to talk on the phone all the time, and he was going to go over to study math, which had been giving him trouble.

"The hell you are!" his dad yelled.

Bob looked for Doreen the next day at school, but he never saw her again.

He had a friend who was also named Bob whose older brothers were in a band. Sometimes on the weekends, the two Bobs would go down to Provo Park to hear the band play. There'd be all kinds of hippies hanging out, playing music. Bob liked the guitarists especially. He'd study their hands and try to imitate what he saw on his own guitar later at home.

One night in seventh grade, he slept over at his buddy Bob's house with a few other guys and they all smoked weed. Bob had never done that before.

Then they went to go break in to the pool

at the Claremont, a big hotel nearby that was painted white.

The world was a swirling thing, and as they walked down the street, Bob realized that, to get there, they'd have to pass right by his mom's house.

He stopped. He didn't want his mom to see him. He didn't want her figuring out he was high. His friends told him he was making a big deal out of nothing, but he turned back alone.

Would his dad know he'd gotten high?

Where was his life headed?

After a long time, his friends finally returned.

The next day his dad asked why his eyes were so red, and Bob said he had hay fever.

He ate acid for the first time later that year with the other Bob and some other friends. They smoked dope and hashish, too, and then rode their bikes up to Tilden Park, a big nature preserve on the crest of the Berkeley Hills with groves of eucalyptus trees.

His bike's tires created huge craters in the earth. The light that came through the trees had been produced in the belly of the sun.

Below, they saw a man and a woman on a tennis court and a bright ball that went one way and then back again.

The ball was as magnificent as the sun.

"Hit the ball! Hit the baaaaall!"

It was Bob who was shouting at them. The others joined in.

"Hit the baaaaaaaall!" they screamed.

A cop had just walked by, but nobody could

tell where they were shouting from. For about an hour they laughed, laughed until their lungs were sore and they were totally lost. Later they found themselves.

Bob lied when his dad asked where he had been.

For his freshman year, Bob went to this strict and boring private high school, then switched back to public school for his sophomore year. As he and the other Bob discussed, that was where the chicks were, and the music, and the drugs.

That first morning at Berkeley High, he got there kind of late. A long line stretched out of the gymnasium. Bob got in the back. He didn't recognize a soul.

Finally, up walked the other Bob. He produced a J and shared it, describing all the great classes he'd just scored. The line inched forward.

Finally, Bob was inside. Different teachers were seated behind tables with signs that said what they taught. Bob walked up to table after table, and they all said they were full, full. He felt like such a loser. At last one teacher smiled at him, and Bob signed up for his class, which it turned out was black history.

When classes started, Bob realized he was basically the only white kid in a lot of shit classes again. Again it was Africa, Africa, slavery, slavery. If they read a book, it was something he'd read in fourth grade at his old school, like *Lord of the Flies*. His grades were as bad as ever.

He did like his acting class. He befriended a few guys in it, this barefoot heroin addict named Paul who wrote poetry and a couple other

27

FREAKS. At lunch they'd get on their bikes and cut. They'd always cut on Tuesdays, which was when the hippies down in Provo Park would pass out the posters for whichever show was coming up that weekend.

There was a crawl space in Bob's closet that he'd painted black. He hung the posters in there. He liked to go in and hang out and admire their psychedelic swirls, remember all the great shit he'd seen. Purple Earthquake, the Quicksilver Messenger Service, Lazarus, Creedence, Big Brother and the Holding Company. At the end of his sophomore year, he got to see his favorite artist, his idol, Jimi Hendrix, at the Berkeley Community Theatre.

He had heard Hendrix for the first time that same year. He'd been tripping at a friend's house, and "Voodoo Chile" had come on the radio.

Those first wobbly licks were really all it took.

From that day forward, Hendrix was his god.

Bob was getting pretty good at guitar. He played his first two real gigs soon after he turned sixteen. He had this friend Dave who lived near his mom's house, and sometimes they'd jam.

One night he and Dave were picked up by a van and driven down to some part of Oakland Bob didn't know. Bob was sort of freaked but just got really stoned, and they began to play.

Now and then he'd glance up: the room was getting full, full of a lot of big dudes wearing leather. Maybe they were Hells Angels. He tried to keep himself calm. He focused on his fingers and on the song.

At three A.M. his amp blew.

The black mass jittered, silenced, and turned.

Bob froze.

He wondered whether the Angels were going to kidnap him and hold him for ransom. He feared they knew his dad was rich and powerful.

Somehow, despite the commotion and being so exhausted and high, he got out to the street and found a ride back to Berkeley.

As they drove in the dark, he slowly clenched and unclenched his sore fingers and felt a rare pride. When he walked in, his dad was still awake. He was furious, but Bob didn't even scream back. He felt great.

One weird thing, he noticed twenty years later, was that the version of "Radar Love" they played that night seemed awfully similar to a song that came out decades later called "We Are the Champions," by Queen. One riff was the same, at least; he remembered the one he'd played because he'd made a mistake.

That show had apparently gone well enough that he was asked soon after to play a house party in Berkeley.

This time, though, he got a little too high and his amps were a little too loud and a neighbor called the cops.

Bob had ruined everything. He slunk out and walked home kicking pinecones and muttering "fuck" while the stars above swirled one way and then the next.

Sometimes he got sad like this when he was high. He wondered what the point of it all was.

His dad was always pissed at him—pissed about his music being too loud, pissed about his grades. Bob would yell that his music mattered more than learning about the slave trade, and his dad would yell back that the Rolling Stones would be dead from drugs in a year and everyone would forget their crappy music.

His dad had a new girlfriend, Pat, who wasn't half bad, at least. His dad had asked Bob a while back whether it'd be alright if he started looking for a new wife, and Bob had said okay. Pat was fun. She'd done some nice things for Bob, like rented him a keyboard and driven him once over to the coast, where he'd gotten to ride a buggy on the dunes.

His dad had also hired this old black lady to cook for them and clean. Her name was Merna. Bob mostly refused to eat her meat loaf sandwiches and pot roast dinners. He worried if his classmates found out he came from the kind of family who had a black maid, they'd kill him.

THEN IT HAPPENED:

One afternoon, he was running through the hallway of Berkeley High on his way to the bathroom. The bell had rung; he'd be late to class. He wasn't running because he cared about that. He was running because he really had to piss. As he ran, he nearly tripped on his jeans, and his hair flapped behind him like a great yellow sheet.

He didn't like going to the bathroom, because that was where especially bad stuff tended to happen—somebody would corner him, rob him. This one guy tried to stab him with a syringe, it was maybe full of ANGEL DUST. And a couple of times someone karate-chopped him in the neck to see if he would pass out, which wasn't hard to do because he was really weak these days. He'd hardly been eating lunch since his dad had taken away his allowance for smoking weed.

He was nearly to the bathroom when he saw the kid, the kid whose fault this all was.

The kid was about as wide as the door he was blocking and probably had six inches on Bob. Bob skidded to a halt, and the kid's eyes widened. With a grin and a glance to his friends, he held out a palm.

"Got a dime?" he asked.

Snickers.

"I said got a dime?"

"Nah, man—" Bob started to say. What was this guy even asking him?

"Price to piss is a dime," the kid said, and his friends laughed.

Bob tried to push by, but the kid reared back and landed his fist in Bob's skinny gut. Bob's arms flailed on the kid's back, and he could smell his sweat, and you know how time moves fast when you're fighting.

As they trudged to the principal's office, Bob knew it wouldn't matter that the kid was bigger and had started it. Bob knew he would get the blame because that's how this place worked. The principal let Bob use his bathroom, then sat the two boys down.

Through the blinds, the day was bright.

The principal asked them what the problem had been. He wore glasses that shone.

31

The kid started saying how he had no idea why Bob had lost it. Kept saying "sir." Bob studied the parking lot. He knew the kid's friends would be out there after school, waiting for him. They'd rough him up, continue searching for their dime. He could practically see the glimmer of their knives. The principal was nodding and the kid was still telling lies. Bob thought about just smashing through the window and running away forever, never hearing any more shit about how white people were to blame for everything, never being taunted and cornered and afraid for his life every day.

Bob was standing now and screaming THIS FUCKING NIGGER WOULD LET ME PEE UNLESS I GAVE HIM A DIME and IM SICK OF YOU FUCKERS and I HOPE YOU ALL GET JKILLED and the principal was standing now, too.

"We do not need your type in this school!" the principal spat, his eyes like embers behind the glass. He gave Bob a slip of paper and told him to get it signed in the office.

The kid who'd started it was let go without punishment, nothing.

Freed like a fish tossed back in a lake.

Bob didn't bother stopping by the office. He stomped out the doors of Berkeley High and began the long steep walk back to the condo.

It was an odd thing to walk home like this in the middle of the day.

Reminded him of a year before.

That afternoon he'd been sitting in class when someone had come on the loudspeaker just after lunch and told them classes were canceled. They were all free to go home.

Bob didn't know what was going on.

He certainly didn't care.

He got on his bike.

It was a beautiful day, as days often are in Berkeley.

As he rode, he realized he was part of a growing crowd, one that he now also realized was cresting toward a line of National Guardsmen. They carried big guns and wore two-nosed rubber masks that made their faces alien and all the same.

Bob dismounted.

Whatever was going on had nothing to do with him, but he didn't know who to tell. He saw a guy pick up a rock and watched it arc through the air—noise and smoke and bullets whizzing.

Bob was sprinting now, dragging his bike.

Glass cascaded and cars burned and everywhere people were falling and crying. Usually, everything is ordered and you don't even notice it, and now everything wasn't, like someone had shaken the fish tank that was the world. A helicopter overhead; gas in the air.

He couldn't see or breathe.

He had fallen into something sharp, a hedge.

He was there a long time, maybe.

Something soft was touching his forehead.

A woman's hand.

"Here," she said, and water spilled down his temples.

He tried to thank her.

At some point he recovered himself and walked all the way to his dad's condo. Up above the tree line, the day was orange and hazy, and downtown was obscured, like the whole place had been cleared by fire.

His dad drove up not long after, parked his car with a lurch, said he couldn't be on campus that day.

BERKELEY WAS A MESS: The Black Panthers marched on campus with rifles. Drugs were everywhere. The hippies hated the vets, and the vets hated the war, and the Hells Angels wanted to go to 'Nam and kill everyone.

His dad was pissed, of course, that Bob had been kicked out of high school. Each morning before he left for work he'd bark at Bob to stay in his room.

At night now Bob could hear his dad and Pat worrying through the walls of the condo about what to do with him. Most days now Bob sat and looked out his bedroom window. This condo was even farther up the Berkeley Hills and had even more incredible views than the house where his mom and sisters still lived.

He watched the fog burn off.

He watched the Bay Bridge gleam and dump its traffic into the white buildings of San Francisco. From way up here, the bridges were like electrical wires, and the sailboats were as small as motes of dust.

In the afternoons, he watched as the sky purpled and the fog commuted back in toward Berkeley. Headlights appeared on the bridge—a streak of red, a streak of white.

He was embarrassed that he had nothing to do all day, and mad at his dad and the principal and the kid whose fault this all was. Truth was, though, he'd take his bedroom and boredom over the hazardous halls of Berkeley High.

Jimi Hendrix hadn't graduated from high school, either, for fuck's sake.

Sometimes as he sat he would think about his favorite place in the world. Back before the divorce had ruined everything, back when his family was still a family, they used to drive every summer to his mom's family's cottage on a lake in Minnesota called L'Homme Dieu.

These were drives that took forever, especially if they went on a side trip to the Grand Canyon or something. He and his sisters were always fussy and sick of each other by the time they began seeing familiar things— the streets of Alexandria, the place with the trampolines, the statue of Ole the Viking that stood nearly thirty feet tall in the center of town. Their car bumbled down the dirt lane, and Bob caught a glimmer of water through the birch green.

And then there was the whole lake and the little white cottage with its lattice skirts. Grandma Mary rushed out from it shouting, "They're here!" and everyone was upon them. Arms outstretched and tails wagged and his dad honked the car's horn for a little too long. They slung open heavy doors and unfurled their legs.

Cousin Tommy came running up from the water, sandy and grinning. He was Bob's best friend at the lake. Looking back on his whole life, Bob

would reflect that these moments in particular—
arriving at Lake L'Homme Dieu at the beginning
of each summer—were some of the happiest. The
water, the embraces, the kisses, all made THE
PLACE TO SEEM KIND OF A MIRRACULAS PARADISE.

He rose early in the morning and crept quietly
from the cottage. He flipped over a canoe on
the shore. Big iron-colored daddy longlegs
stumbled across the wet sand. The shallow water
wasn't yet warmed by the sun, and he violated
its calm with his strokes. Out on the point,
he'd look at the eagle's nest, see if he could
spot the chicks.

He spent as much time as he could out on
the water. He'd take out the rowboat that had
a little engine, trawling for pike or bass.
Sometimes he'd drop an anchor and catch sunfish
or perch.

Sometimes he'd take his catch down to a
neighbor, MR. PEIERY, this dude who lived with
two old girlfriends. HE SEEMED OUT OF THE PAST
SO I FIGURED HIM FOR A PIRATE OR SOMETHING:

Mr. Peiery had the most wonderful seashell
collection. It gathered dust on bookshelves and
windowsills, orbs and spirals unlike any Bob
had ever seen. He claimed he'd found them right
there at the lake. Strange thing was, years
later, Bob saw a collection he could have sworn
was Mr. Peiery's in a San Francisco museum. How
a museum could have gotten ahold of it, he had
no idea.

Summer days were long. The adults lounged on
the shore, napped and read books. The teenage

girls—his older sister, Heather, and his cousin Jane—tanned and swam. Jane even swam across the whole lake once, with a boat following her for safety. His little sister, Debbie, would squat in the shallows, playing with the minnows. His cousin Tommy read a lot of comic books, and he and Bob would play Wiffle Ball or badminton on the lawn.

Some afternoons were spent trying to get everybody up on water skis. Bob was pretty good. His cousin David, Tommy's older brother, was the best of the kids. As he passed by the dock, David could turn up a ski to spray everyone on the dock. Their uncle Rollin was so good he could kick off one ski, fold his free leg across the other, and put one hand behind his head, as if he were relaxing on a beachside chair. Everyone would point and chuckle and applaud.

Rollin was his mom's brother and everybody's favorite. He was always making up silly things to do. One time he packed all the kids into the car, rolled the windows down, told them to laugh really loud, and drove into town. The kids laughed and laughed, and the people of Alexandria, going about their days, wondered what in the world?, which only made them laugh more. Sometimes Rollin would pack them into the trunk and sneak them into the drive-in. Once the movie had started and the guy had come by to spray for bugs, they would emerge like circus clowns and sit on the roof.

Grandpa Ray had hurt his back when he was younger, so he couldn't do much. Once a summer they all put on formal clothes and Grandpa Ray

treated them to a steak dinner at the golf course—
best steaks on the planet, as far as Bob was
concerned. Grandma Mary spent her days inside the
little white cottage, cleaning, cooking three
meals a day for everybody. Only later did Bob
realize how hard Grandma Mary must have worked.
She kept a jar of her enormous sugar cookies on
a low shelf in the kitchen. Throughout the day,
children would sneak in, take one, and sprint
across the lawn, once more to the lake.

A big summer rainstorm occasionally blew
through during the afternoon, and they'd all
be cooped up inside. He'd play cribbage with
his grandpa and uncle Rollin. He'd read comics
with Tommy; they had an incredible collection,
one Bob regretted they didn't keep better track
of through the years.

When night fell at the lake, Bob and Tommy
would whisper to each other. Once they shared
what they wanted to be when they grew up.

Tommy said he wanted to work with computers,
which was strange to Bob because he didn't know
if computers had been invented yet.

Bob told Tommy he wanted to be a rock star.

They whispered good night.

Through the cottage's thin walls, Bob could
hear his family shift and breathe. He could hear
bugs outside buzzing and the loons finishing
their night song and Bob felt about as free and
happy as he ever would.

Not long after he was kicked out of Berkeley
High, Bob was sitting in his bedroom one morning,

staring out his window like always, when there was a knock at his door. His dad and his dad's girlfriend, Pat, stood in the hall.

"What's up?" Bob asked.

"Bob," his dad said, "pack a bag."

"Why?"

"I said pack a bag."

"Where we going?" Bob asked.

There was a pause. Pat and his dad looked at each other.

"A real fun place," Pat answered, and her lipstick smiled. They stared at him.

"Where?"

"Don't worry," his dad said.

They shut his door. Bob got on his belly and retrieved a suitcase from beneath his bed.

He figured they were going up to Tahoe. His dad had bought a vacation home up there back around when the divorce began. It was about a four-hour drive away, just over the Nevada border.

If the place up at Tahoe was meant to be a replacement for the cottage on Lake L'Homme Dieu, it didn't come close. When they went up there, Bob—and his sisters, if his dad had them, too—had to sleep in a dark room. His dad would go out to the casino with whoever he was dating, maybe come home late. His dad had dated this one woman for a while who had little kids. Bob had to babysit and spent the night chasing them around like he was a monster.

Bob lugged his suitcase into the hall. His dad and Pat were waiting with their own suitcases by the door.

Pat walked out to the car while his dad locked up, and Bob followed. He realized this might be a good moment to ask her about something that had been bothering him, which was what had happened the other night.

It had started when his dad had come home and told Bob he was having a graduation party for his students. He told Bob to put on his pajamas and stay in his room.

"It's the middle of the day!" Bob protested.

"You do as you're told!" his dad barked.

Bob slammed his door.

EVERTHING HIT ME AT ONCE THAT NIGHT: He had no money. He had no friends. He was so thin, so hungry. Reflecting on the past year, the only good thing that had happened to him was he had discovered Jimi Hendrix.

He picked up his guitar. His calloused fingers spidered up and down the frets and he got lost in the sound.

Some hours later, he tuned back in to the noise on the other side of the door. He could make out chatter and square music. He stepped onto the landing. The party was much larger than he'd expected.

"What's this?" someone said.

A sea of boozy glasses turned toward him, and at its center was his dad's red face.

"I thought I told you to stay in your room!" his dad shouted.

Bob retreated. He shut his door behind him again and grasped his guitar by its body and neck.

Then someone opened his door.

He figured it was his dad there to yell at him again, but it wasn't; it was Pat. She held a finger in front of her lips like this was their secret. She had some guy with her, and a bottle of wine and three glasses. The guy, it turned out, was a musician, which was why Pat had wanted them to meet.

She knelt on the carpet and poured them all some wine.

"Play us a song," she said to Bob. He sat at the keyboard and did. Pat smiled and so did the guy, who then picked up Bob's guitar and repeated the melody.

"Whoa, man," Bob exclaimed.

"I guess it's catchy," the guy said. Years later, Bob would hear that same tune in a radio hit and wonder whether this guy, whose name he'd forgotten, had lifted it from him.

Bob told them about his dream of becoming a rock star and about how recently he'd played his first two gigs—the one in Oakland with the Hells Angels, and the house party in Berkeley. As they chatted and played, Bob thought about how this was one of the nicest things that had ever happened to him, Pat introducing him to this other musician and letting him have some wine.

Next thing he knew, he awoke.

A bright morning.

He blinked.

He looked at his hand, which was hanging off the side of the bed and still clutching a glass.

He put it down and sat up.

Had he fallen asleep?

Or gotten drunk?

Had he embarrassed himself in front of Pat and the musician?

Bob wanted to ask Pat about it now, as he set his suitcase in the trunk beside hers, but his dad had already caught up. He'd have to wait until later. Whatever had happened, at least it had been their secret.

Bob sat in the backseat, and they pulled away. He looked at his dad's hands on the wheel and Pat's folded on her knee.

At some point, he noticed they weren't headed east on the freeway, as they would have if they were driving up to Tahoe, but were instead going into downtown Berkeley. Maybe they were running an errand before they hit the road.

They pulled into a lot and parked.

His dad and Pat got out of the car.

"Come on, Bob," his dad said to him through the cracked window. Pat had opened the trunk and was lifting out Bob's suitcase. She had nice arms, from tennis.

"What are we doing here, Dad?"

His dad opened Bob's door. Bob noticed that Pat looked—perhaps had looked this whole time—really upset.

"Come on, Bob," his dad repeated.

It couldn't have been more than thirty feet between that parking spot and the entrance of Herrick Hospital.

Thirty or so feet of asphalt shining in the Berkeley sun.

42

Thirty or so feet that probably took under twenty seconds to cross, even with a suitcase and confusion. There were planters of ivy and irises. A redwood tree.

Bob did not realize the importance of those twenty seconds.

He did not try to escape.

Escape may have meant that he would have led a life according to his own free will, a thing that he, like any of us, assumed he had all along.

He summarized the life he lived instead on his manuscript's cover page, which, for whatever reason, was the only page he didn't type in all caps:

IM ROBERT

this is a true story of a boy brought up in berkeley california durring the sixties and seventies who was unable to identify with reality and there for labeled as a psychotic paranoid schizophrenic for the rest of his life;

The Way Society Was

Any family is, in a sense, a cluster of individuals bound together by love and money and contracts and genetic material—individuals who sometimes fail to resemble one another in significant ways. And any two individuals, of course, will perceive and remember totally different versions of the same events.

As once-related people go, my grandparents are two especially inclined to see things differently. When I interviewed them about their son, they were in their mid-eighties. They had been divorced for many decades. Though they didn't live far apart—only about fifteen minutes, driving—I cannot tell you if, in my lifetime, I've ever seen the two in the same room.

My grandfather Gene lived with his second wife, Agnes, in a ritzy town in a large home atop a hill. When you rang the bell, it echoed throughout the cavernous inside—all white carpets and stairways—and their little white dogs yapped about. Gene had worked a long and lauded career and retired in the early nineties a wealthy man. He'd always seemed nice but was quiet. His slacks were ironed, and he ordered his martinis with vodka. He was very smart, it was clear, and he'd sometimes betray a wit.

It was Agnes who always did more of the talking on their behalf, Agnes who signed their Christmas and birthday cards and checks. She had her hair done regularly at a salon and wore gold jewelry. She was proper and serious, the only member of my family who'd correct me if, for example, I ended a sentence with a preposition.

My grandma Marilyn lived in a suburb deeper in the East Bay. Every house on her block was the same shade of tan. She had never remarried. If anything, she seemed proud of how frugally she lived. She had driven the same powder blue Toyota since the mid-eighties. She'd brag that sometimes people would stop her in parking lots and ask to buy it, and she'd say no sir. She had a head of white hair and skin that was leathery and cut up from time working in her yard. She was so short she came up to my chest when we hugged, and I'm not tall.

Marilyn was goofy, friendly, a sort of amazingly effortless pianist. When I'd go to see her, we'd leash her big stubborn golden retriever and walk around the cul-de-sacs. She'd describe which houses contained dogs or people who were her friends. Marilyn has always loved stories, listening to them and telling them, even though her own memory never seemed that great.

The accounts Gene and Marilyn each gave me of their marriage and its failure had little in common. Same with their accounts of what happened to their son. Generally speaking, people on Gene's side of the family offered recollections and opinions that were similar to his, and people on Marilyn's had versions more like hers. People on both sides went out of their way to tell me why I wasn't to trust those on the other. I'd receive evidence in the mail: letters, photocopies of ancient paperwork with fresh notes scrawled in the margins.

My mom has never been close with either side of her family, nor especially impolite. It was for this reason that our nuclear family had always been one of the rare groups who could leap with impunity across that fault line. Growing up, I'd observed how full of ire so many of the people in her family seemed to be about old events. So many had stayed mad for so long, and I, at least, never really understood why.

:::::

My grandparents did agree that Bob, as a boy, had been happy.

"Healthy and happy and active," Gene said.

Great at sports, whatever he tried.

Not that Gene recalled many specifics from Bob's childhood. He worked very hard back then, he explained, sometimes coming home for dinner and returning immediately to the office. He did remember the time he taught his son to ride a bike. Bob wasn't like other kids, where you have to hold on and run alongside. "He got on and just rode away," Gene said.

Bob had been born at a naval hospital in South Carolina back when Gene was still in the service. The family had then relocated to Minnesota, where my grandparents are from.

Gene had done everything in his life right and was always at the top of his class. In the late fifties, he was hired by the University of California at Berkeley, and the family moved west. He was considered quite young to have gotten such a prestigious job. Berkeley was one of the biggest public schools in the nation and, many felt, the best.

They lived those first few years in a house down near campus and then moved to a bigger one up in the Berkeley Hills, a stucco four-bedroom with incredible views. There were the three kids and the family dogs, and on Christmas morning there'd be so much wrapping paper and tinsel that you couldn't see the carpet.

They entertained. "University people," Marilyn called their friends.

As for how she spent her time, she cared for the children, cooked, cleaned, starched shirts. She guffawed, remembering that life: "I hated starching shirts."

Bob did Boy Scouts. He went to Sunday school at a nearby Methodist Church. His elementary school was well regarded and, like their neighborhood, almost entirely white.

As in many American cities, this didn't reflect the overall composition of the town, which by 1960 was almost 20 percent black (a figure that had nearly doubled since 1950). In Berkeley, as in much of America, black families seeking to rent or buy houses in desirable neighborhoods like the Berkeley Hills faced routine discrimination. Berkeley's black residents mostly lived in two neighborhoods down near the Oakland border.

In 1963, a coalition of liberals had attempted to pass an anti-discrimination bill, but it narrowly failed. That was when they'd turned to the schools, devising one of the most ambitious and progressive integration programs to date in the United States. In 1964, to the shock of many, it passed. The plan, though, allowed for four years before elementary schoolers would be bused, during which time many white families moved to suburbs farther east. One of my uncle's friends whose family moved around then described it as an "exodus."

I asked Gene whether he considered moving the family. He replied that school integration "was never a big deal in Berkeley. At least none that I knew about."

As often happened when I spoke with my grandfather, I couldn't tell if he truly didn't remember or if he was just disinclined to talk. I'd guess that, like a lot of white people, he was unaccustomed to being asked direct questions about race. He seemed likewise not that interested in other questions I asked about events happening in Berkeley during those years.

I'd heard before, for example, that Gene had been involved in a fairly famous dispute between the university and a student activist group called the Free Speech Movement, or FSM. During the fall semester of 1964, a group of Berkeley students who'd just come back from volunteering during the Freedom Summer in the South began to protest a ban against political speech on the university's campus. These students set up card tables and began distributing pamphlets and fund-raising for black civil rights. When one student was arrested, hundreds and then thousands of people surrounded the cop car he'd been put in, and for seventy-two hours, they sat there. As the semester wore on, the FSM organized further protests and eventually staged the largest mass arrest in the history of the state. I'd heard before that Gene was one of the professors asked to adjudicate the disciplinary hearings for FSM members.

He didn't have much to say about the experience. He did his job, he said.

I asked how he felt about the fight they were having, and he admitted that he found the whole thing kind of "foolish," as if the students wanted one thing one day and something else the next. "Sort of a pain in the butt," he said.

The thing about the FSM—the reason they are written about in history books—is that they won their fight. They were a small ragtag organization. Somehow, they pressured the University of California Regents—a body always thusly capitalized, one made up of some of the most rich and powerful people in the state, one that reports to the governor himself—to capitulate.

Suddenly, on Berkeley's campus, speech was free.

It was an event some historians credit with sparking, at least in part, the greater cultural conflagration called "the Sixties."

It was sometime around then, 1964, that the children of the baby boom, that great slumbering mass, started waking up. They started growing out their hair. They traded their slacks for jeans. They took off their panty hose, their bras. Many left behind their families and their hometowns and whatever those places meant. When they did—when they tuned in and dropped out—a lot of them drove west. They showed up in little towns like the one I'm from, or they went more rural, to communes. A lot of them went to San Francisco, to the Haight, and even more went to Berkeley. Tens of thousands of young people, non-students, moved to the area around Telegraph Avenue during the latter half of the decade. The streets were flooded with them and their flesh and their dress and their strange-smelling smoke and their strange-sounding music and their sludge of demands. They wanted peace. They wanted love. They wanted freedom, equality. They wanted to save Mother Earth.

Everybody was in Berkeley—artists and celebrities and deadbeats. There were the anarchists over in Provo Park, there were the newly proclaimed gods of the Bay Area sound. The Hells Angels showed up, as they often did in turbulent places back then, like wasps to hot trash.

The Black Panthers were founded in neighboring Oakland by Bobby Seale and Huey Newton, who met at nearby Merritt Community College. The Panthers wanted fair housing, good schools. They wanted to end police brutality. They wrote a list of ten demands that their members could memorize and recite. "We want freedom," it began. "We want the power to determine the destiny of our black community."

There were so many followers of so many gurus in Berkeley, so many participants in so many revolutions, so many believers in so many manifestos and sacred texts. A lot of these factions disagreed with one another about a lot, but over time many found they could agree that they hated the war. As the decade wore on, massive anti-war protests were held in town.

Gene said he read about whatever was happening on Telegraph or in Washington or Vietnam in the paper, same as everyone else. He explained that he and his colleagues were a world away, up on campus.

One time, though, a kid did break into his office, he said. They must have started bombing Cambodia, because the kid was shouting: "They're bombing Cambodia! You have to stop them!"

Gene seemed to chuckle, but then paused. "They felt very strongly," he said in his straightforward way.

Like his son, he remembered the day the situation in town finally boiled over, the riots in May 1969, what historians call "Bloody Thursday." The dispute was ostensibly about a university-owned parking lot that some hippies had rather randomly co-opted and declared a park for the people. Someone had put a notice in the popular hippie newspaper, *The Berkeley Barb*, advertising a People's Park work party at the parking lot. Many showed up, unrolling lawns and planting flowers.

Authorities then seized and chained up the parking lot. When the hippies tried to take it back, Governor Ronald Reagan called in the National Guard. (Some commentators felt he had won his 1967 bid for governor in part because of his promise to "clean up the mess at Berkeley.")

For seventeen days, the Guard occupied Berkeley. Congregations were broken up and banned. By many accounts, the countercultural spirit was never really the same.

Gene remembered trucks spraying tear gas passed right by his office; why they were on campus, he didn't know. He had to close the windows.

I asked what he thought of that.

"Not very good," he said. "The stuff stinks."

I had wanted to ask Gene about these events because, since reading Bob's account, I wondered whether what happened between him and Bob had been a cultural misunderstanding. I thought about the phrase Bob had typed on his manuscript's cover page, identify with reality, and I wondered what reality even was at that time. I pictured this father and son—one in his creased slacks, the other tripping on his long jeans—on continents drifting apart.

A lot of Bob's friends talked about the fighting at school; some talked about how they understood what integration was all about only later. They remembered Bob got picked on, guessed it was because he was small and so blond.

My uncle's friend whose name was also Bob told me about a time when he and my uncle were teenagers, driving around in a car with four other guys. There were six of them and only two names between them. "It was four Daves and two Bobs," the other Bob said. "That was the time we were in. We were trying to break out of that. That's what the drugs were about. That's what the rebellion against our parents was about." He said he and my uncle were "psychedelic partners."

Another of my uncle's friends—someone who hadn't seen or heard from him since high school—wanted to hear all about what had happened through the course of Bob's life. After I answered his questions, I asked whether the truth surprised him. "I think those were tough times for all of us," he said, "just because of the way society was."

Gene didn't seem very bothered by his son's interest in hippie things, the crawl space he'd painted black, for example, or the loud music. He did recall being frustrated by Bob's poor academic performance. The problem, he said, was that Bob just wouldn't go to school.

He recalled that Bob showed improvement the year he went to private school, and that Bob had later said to him he felt it was an error to transfer. "He wanted to go back to Berkeley High. He has said that he thinks that was a terrible mistake." Gene couldn't remember whether Bob was expelled from high school (and our attempts to obtain Bob's school records weren't successful). Gene did recall that his son never got along with "the blacks" but said he didn't know why.

He didn't know back then that his son was doing drugs, said he never smelled marijuana on him or anything. He didn't remember taking away his allowance for smoking weed. In general, he did not remember fighting nearly as much as Bob described.

Gene talked about how difficult it was, raising Bob alone on top of everything else. He guessed that Bob probably would have preferred to stay with his mom and sisters. But the problem was that Bob and Marilyn were always fighting. One time she dumped all his stuff in the middle of the street.

I asked what they fought about.

"She just hated men, I think, for some reason," he said. "I did it to her, something. Anyway, she would pick on Bob. She would go ape, and she would pick on Bob and throw him out."

Marilyn didn't recall fighting with her son as much as he or Gene described.

If she and Bob did argue, it was because he was always trying to get her to reconcile with Gene. And that wasn't going to happen. It was a pretty radical thing to do, in 1968, go to an attorney and say you wanted to divorce your lauded professor husband.

"I made my decision to be independent and that I could do it," she said. She had her reasons, though she didn't want to go into them.

Bob wouldn't accept it, though; he kept pushing her to reconcile. That's why, finally, "I just said, 'Well, if you feel that comfortable with him, then go live with him.'"

She talked about how hard it was already, with the two girls, and said the judge had made her get work right away. She took a course to brush up her shorthand. She got a job at a hotel, then as a secretary in the superintendent's office for the Oakland Public Schools. Her boss was Dr. Marcus Foster, the district's first black superintendent (who was later assassinated by members of a terrorist organization that next and, more famously, kidnapped the heiress Patty Hearst).

Marilyn's house became the kind of place where kids were always hanging out—her daughters, their friends. She rented Bob's room to some university girls to make extra money, and then she built out an apartment downstairs. Her niece Jane from Minnesota got pregnant in Morocco and came to have her baby there. There was an exchange student from Japan. The girls would dress up in old clothing and take silly pictures; they'd brush lemon juice in their hair and lie out on the porch in the sun. Someone at some point hung a sign in a window saying UFOs were welcome to land there.

Marilyn lost all her friends in the divorce, but she made new ones she liked better. Her life began when she divorced, she told me. I don't get the sense that she's ever regretted what she did, leaving Gene.

She also spent, I think, a lifetime wondering how things might have been different.

"If Bob had stayed there with me," she said, "I don't know what would have happened."

THE CAGED
WINDOW

His dad handed the clipboard back to the woman behind the glass.

"What's going on here, Dad?" Bob asked.

Someone grabbed Bob's arm—a man wearing white. He was tying a BRACELETT around Bob's wrist.

"We're going to Tahoe," said Pat. Pat still looked really upset. "Have a good time," she said to Bob, her voice small.

His dad put his hands in his trouser pockets. He turned to Pat.

"What am I doing here, Dad?" Bob asked. "What's going on?"

His dad looked at Bob and nodded. Pat took his dad's arm.

"Stay here, Bob," his dad said. The man in white let go of his wrist.

"When will you come back?" Bob asked.

"Soon."

They walked out the doors, to the car, to a week at the lake.

"Follow me," said the man. Bob still looked back through the doors at the parking lot.

He followed the man onto an elevator. Guy was tall, muscular. He said nothing. The doors parted. They stepped out and proceeded down a long hallway, passing doors and nurses. At the end of the hall was a thick glass window and behind it were men.

Some were white and some were black. Some were young but all seemed old. Some were jittery and some were still. Some moved deliberately, others as if piloted by a puppeteer hidden up in the humming lights. Most wore long hair and beards. Most were smoking. Every single one of them wore pajamas.

"Wait here," the man said, and Bob watched his white cuffs walk away.

One of the guys in pajamas was staring at Bob through the glass. He had stringy hair and big glasses.

Why was he staring at Bob?

Did Bob know him?

Did he have some sort of problem?

A black woman was standing next to him now, a nurse. "Follow me," she said.

She took out a ring of keys and unlocked a heavy door. Together they entered the room behind the glass, a space Bob would later know to call an open ward. It was artificially bright. He followed her down another hall. She stopped and unlocked another door.

"Hang your clothes in this closet." She pointed.

Bob said nothing.

"You know what a hanger is, boy?"

"Yeah, I do!"

"Don't get smart with me," she snapped. "Wait outside your room when you're done."

"What for?" he asked.

She shut the door.

Why wouldn't he know what a hanger was?

There were folded pajamas on one of the two bare mattresses. There was a little window with bars on it. Outside the sun shone. Outside it was just a day and his dad and Pat were driving up to Tahoe.

There must have been some kind of mistake.

He went back into the hall. Doctors in coats stood behind the glass, their voices inaudible, clipboards in hand. One of them was a bearded black man. Bob tried to get his attention.

"What am I supposed to do?" Bob shouted.

The guy seemed to notice but didn't react. He continued writing. Maybe he couldn't hear through the glass?

"What am I supposed to do?" Bob shouted again.

The guy definitely noticed Bob this time, but again did nothing.

Now Bob screamed: WHAT AM I SPOSED TO DO YOU FUCKING MONKEY?

The guy picked up a phone. The heavy door opened and two orderlies stomped out and put their hands on him. As he fell, Bob saw the same guy with stringy hair and glasses staring at him—why, Bob had no fucking idea. His eyes followed Bob all the way to the floor. There had been some kind of horrible mistake.

"What the fuck!" Bob shouted.

A knee rammed into his back and a hand worked its way under his crotch and pulled at his belt. Fingers slithered down his buttons. Bob writhed and screamed. They tugged off his shoes and jeans and he felt cold on his thighs and chest. He set his chin on the floor. Everyone was watching him now, not just the guy with the stringy hair, everybody was standing around watching him. The orderlies pushed his arms into the pajama top and his legs down into the pants. He swatted and kicked. They grabbed his shoulders and ankles and dragged him through a set of doors onto a different hallway like he was a protestor limp in a cop's arms.

The new hallway was just as bright, but empty. It would have been silent but Bob was screaming. There was a bathroom at the end and three little doors. Each had a little window. A nurse unlocked one.

"What the fuck are you doing?" Bob screamed.

"Don't fight!" someone said as he tried to get them off.

"I'm not!" Bob yelled.

They dragged him onto the cell's cement floor. They loomed over him, a stand of redwoods. One nurse had a syringe.

"I won't fight!" he yelled.

"Something to calm you down—" someone said.

"I'll be calm. I'm okay!" He writhed and screamed, "Why are you doing this?!"

Nobody said a word and the syringe squirted and he screamed, "Does my dad know what you're doing?! Does he? Does he?!" His dad was an important man and he could ruin these people for what they were doing. "I want to see the head nurse!" he screamed. "I demand to see the head nurse!"

They all paused. One of them left the room.

The pajama pants didn't fit him right.

After awhile some old lady wearing a paper hat came in.

"My dad just drove me here—" Bob started to explain.

"Robert," she said, "this is for your own good."

She had a syringe THE SIZE OF A PUSHUP POPSICKLE. The two orderlies wrestled him back onto his stomach.

"Stop shouting!" the old lady shouted. "This is for your own good!" These guys didn't get it; this old lady didn't get it: there had been a mistake.

Then an even worse thought occurred: what if his dad had known this was what was going to happen to him?

This was the worst thing that had ever happened.

This was worse than being cornered in the bathroom at Berkeley High. This was worse than the riot, the bullets and the gas and the glass. This had to be worse than death, he figured, and so he screamed, "Shoot it in my heart!"

He felt the needle puncture the fat of his butt.

:POOR KID: said a voice.

As the needle exited, Bob began to sob. He flapped his arms and thrashed around his head and sobbed. If he could have, he would have pounded straight through the cement floor and landed on the hospital hallway below. Dust and wires and sparks would rain around him and patients on gurneys would shriek as he ran down the hall. He'd run out the glass doors and in front of a bus. He'd be hit and it'd be over. He'd be nothing but a smudge of hair and blood on a windshield. He'd be nothing but some shattered glass on the pavement, there for people to walk by, there until it rained.

He felt the needle enter his other butt cheek now and he wondered what would happen next.

"You'll be okay now," another voice said.

One by one they left the cell and shut the door behind them.

He climbed onto his legs. The door inside had no handle. Through his window, he watched them walk away down the hall, their silhouettes fogged by three inches of glass and the anti-psychotics flooding his brain.

He felt the floor asking him to fall. He swallowed air and screamed at the little window, "Let me out of here!" His scream ricocheted around the cell—its cement floor and walls, its rubber mattress, its one bare bulb overhead. It took all the breath he had but he managed to repeat it, "Let me out of here!" The floor begged him to fall but this was a moment unlike any he'd ever experienced. This day, this cell, this was his Vietnam. This was bullets whizzing from the trees and this was red clouds wafting. This was having to run so hard he didn't even feel the pummeling weight of his pack and his gun. Nobody cared about him—not society, not his family. He was all he had now, so he screamed and screamed and screamed as loud and hard as his drowsy lungs would let.

:::::

The door opened again.

"Relax. You gotta fucking relax," the orderly said. He raised a syringe. Bob tried to fight him, but his hands were wobbly like vines. The needle entered his skin and exited.

The door was again closed.

He crawled across the cement and aboard the plastic mattress.

He flipped onto his back. The bulb was rocking back and forth, slightly at first, but then more, and more.

Maybe he was still yelling; he wasn't sure.

Maybe he was asleep.

Maybe several hours passed, or minutes, or days.

In that cell, that real cell, he pictured a bunny, a fake bunny that was stuffed and yellow and had eyes of yarn X's like it was dead. It belonged to his little sister Debbie.

Bob remembered Debbie clutching the bunny as they pulled into a motel, his still-intact family of five. They were on their way back from Minnesota, somewhere on the edge of the Midwest and the Great Plains. His dad registered them in the office while his mom huffed and got out of the car. Through the glass the kids could hear them yelling again into one another's faces; they'd been fighting non-stop this whole drive back from Minnesota. His mom glared up at his dad with hands on her hips and then opened the doors to the backseat.

"Get out, get out," his mom said. Heather stood with one hip cocked to the side, frowning at the pavement. She was about thirteen. Bob was eleven; Debbie still in elementary school.

"Help your sister with the luggage," his mom said to Bob. Debbie, with her bunny, slid out of the backseat, trailed by her milky hair.

Next to the motel, they found a swing beneath a wind-swept pine, its single seat cut from an old tire. Debbie sat and kicked out her feet. Heather and Bob stood next to her. Neither was going to push. They were all sad. Sad to have left Lake L'Homme Dieu, and their cousins, and to be left with their parents' screams.

Debbie pumped her feet out and swung a little higher, bunny riding on her lap.

Through the motel's wooden walls, they could hear the fight, though it was hard to make out, like prairie thunder so far off you can't quite tell if it's not just a truck rumbling somewhere down the highway. They heard a scream that was their mother's and a booming reply from their dad. *Crackboom*. Debbie scraped her feet along the gravel to a halt. *Crackboom*.

Perhaps the sky itself darkened, a preamble to a spooky mid-August storm, and then, like a rush of rain, their yelling intensified and the hotel manager tried to kick them out.

They'd been in the car about an hour the next day when Bob noticed Debbie wasn't holding her bunny.

"Dad," he said. "Dad."

"Yes, Bob."

"Debbie forgot her bunny."

"Her what?"

"Her bunny. She forgot her bunny—"

"My bunny!" Debbie swung her head all around, looking behind her back and beneath her little thighs.

"Gene, we have to go back—" his mom said.

"You want me to go back for a doll?" his dad shouted.

"Dad, my bunny!" Debbie was sobbing now. "Dad, my bunny!"

The car was silent a while before his dad said, "We'll have it sent."

From above a voice interrupted: "We want you to take these."

Bob's cheek was resting on the floor of the cell. He couldn't make out who was standing overhead. There was a cup next to his face.

He did not move.

He was alone again.

He looked inside the cup; there were pills.

He didn't take them.

He closed his eyes.

He was pretty sure his dad never did what he said, never had that bunny sent.

The door opened. He felt the hands upon him and, his eyes still closed, he screamed. He saw that dead-eyed bunny on the swing pocked with rain, its ears flapping in the rising wind. He saw his dad's red face commanding him back in his room amidst the sea of faces. He heard all the black kids surrounding him shouting *fight fight fight*. The syringe slid cold into his ass. A familiar prick now. And release.

He was alone in the cell.

Half-formed phrases and bits of melodies and objects and faces he'd once seen flashed through his mind like Chinatown cherry bombs exploding in a Berkeley backyard, or heavenly lights descending, or the little sparks he'd get in his eyes if he closed them real tight after looking at the sun on Lake L'Homme Dieu.

His line was lifting a twitching sunfish from the water when the cell door opened again.

"You gotta stop yelling, man," the orderly said. "People are trying to sleep."

Bob looked at the guy and his words came out like half-chewed food.

He couldn't even talk and this asshole says he's yelling.

The next day, maybe, someone came in, looked at him, left.

Maybe there was nothing he could do.

Maybe there was really nothing he could do.

He thought or he dreamed about Lydia Treeantopolis. He pictured her walking up to the stoop and away. He wondered where she had gone.

Someone was lifting him up, hoisting his arm around a shoulder. Guy smelled like cigarettes. He dragged Bob out into the bright corridor. Bob blinked and tried to ask him where they were going.

"Stand up!" he said.

Bob wouldn't or couldn't or both.

The guy dragged him. Each door they passed had a little window. Inside was another Bob, another Bob screaming as Lydia Treeantopolis walked away forever. Why had she come to his house that evening? What had she wanted to tell him?

The orderly unlocked another door. In this one the bed was wooden. There was a towel on a hook. The guy sat him on the bed and left.

This door also had no handle.

He lay on the bed and looked at the ceiling.

He thought about the shrink his dad had made him see, some old dude whose office was on Shattuck Avenue. He kept asking Bob stupid questions off some questionnaire, like what his favorite color was, or did he love his sisters, or was he a rock star.

Dude seemed NUTS to Bob, like he'd never spent a day outside of his office.

HE MADE ME SICK:

Bob studied the stained ceiling and sang: "There must be some kind of way out of here."

The ceiling seemed to listen.

"There must be some kind of way out of here," he repeated, louder this time, letting his throat catch his sound.

Hadn't even been that long ago he saw Jimi live.

How wild that crowd had been, just waiting for him to come on. How they'd panted, the air thick and sweaty and hot with glee. How they'd howled when he finally emerged, with his axe, his kerchief, his sleeves. How they'd moaned when he touched his lips to the microphone's weave and his fingers to those strings. How they shook with the reason of his sound.

Bob sang every song he could remember from that night, tried to remember the whole set.

He sang it as loud as he could, and the stained ceiling became a dark mass of youth, screaming for him.

Then he started crying, and WONDE R WHAT THE TOWEL WAS FOR:

Next they moved him to a room with roommates, older guys. They let him onto the area he'd seen before where people shuffled around, which was called the open ward.

Bob mostly tried to keep to himself, which wasn't hard because whatever they were giving him made him feel like a fish inside a bowl inside a bowl inside a bowl.

He would wake and line up to take pills and eat and then wander around. He'd line up to take more pills and then eat and then wander around until it was time to sleep. He would wake and line up to take pills and so on. These weren't decisions he was making; they were just things he did. There was nobody to fight. There was no reason to live. This, as far as he knew, would be the rest of his life.

The nurses with their carts of syringes would wheel up to him and suck out tubes of his blood and smile and wheel away and he couldn't even get a straight answer to what they needed it all for. Sometimes he would eat and wonder when he last had. Sometimes he'd realize he was sitting on the sofa in the dayroom, in front of the little TV, and he would wonder how long he'd been there. All the time he was concerned that somebody in here was poisoning him.

How strange: one minute you're sitting in

your room watching the world out your bedroom window, and next, this.

Small moments interrupted this monotony. Once, an orderly passing him in the hall said: "You sounded like Hendrix back there."

"Yeah, man?" Bob asked.

"Yeah."

Bob grinned and the guy did, too.

Bob hoped he'd see him again but he never did.

They sometimes let him go outside. He walked blinking onto the asphalt. The first time he did he had a terrible sunburn that night; whatever they were giving him made his skin fry. The next time he went outside he was careful to stand in a sliver of shade.

Some of the orderlies were sharing a joint and gave Bob a toke. Bob said thanks. It was one of the nicest things that had happened to him since he got here, however long that had been.

His doctor was this dude named Dr. G. He was old and always looked at Bob's chart with greater interest than he did Bob himself. Bob would try to get some information about what the hell was going on, and Dr. G. would weasel out of answering. Bob wasn't yet a Christian, not really, but later, when he was, he speculated that Dr. G. had been the devil himself.

"Why am I in here, man?" Bob asked.

"Because we want you to get well," Dr. G. replied, without meeting Bob's eyes.

"When am I getting out?" Bob asked.

"When you are better."

"Better from what?" he asked.

Dr. G. wouldn't answer.

"Better from what?"

Bob asked everybody that question all the time—Dr. G., the nurses, the orderlies—and of course nobody could give him a good answer, which made sense, because this had been a mistake.

Sometimes they'd sit in chairs in a circle called group. The lady in charge wore pants and had big curly hair. One at a time everybody would answer the question of why they were in there.

Bob had never heard stories like these: Men who'd touched their daughters. Men who'd killed their wives. Men who'd come back from war with their heads full of inside-out bodies and what they'd done.

"And you, Bob, why are you in here?" asked the lady in pants.

Bob paused.

He didn't have a story. He'd never touched his daughter; he'd never killed his wife. He was too young to have those things, too young still to even go to war. The one person who could tell him why—Dr. G.—wouldn't and so Bob repeated again and again, "I don't know. I don't know," and he realized the drops of water on the linoleum were his tears.

The others just sat there, probably too focused on their own problems, too fucked up on their own medicine, to feel bad for him.

"Thank you, Robert," said the lady in pants.

He was getting sort of used to the place when he got sick. Not sick in whatever way they were telling him he was already, but sick like weak, with a fiery rash that erupted all over his arms and back. He was screaming at himself in the mirror when the nurses came and laid him down. They found a real doctor, not a hack devil doctor like G. He had German measles, they told him, though they didn't tell him what that meant or whether he would die. They wheeled him into a room with three roommates, who hated him, and then another room where he was alone.

He could feel night.

He could feel day.

Night again.

And so on.

His skin blistered and in his mind he heard ringing. He heard ringing and he thought about that telephone in the hall at his mom's house, the one that the court put in. It would ring sometimes, ring and ring, and nobody would answer. "Let it ring! Let it ring!" his mom would say and sometimes Bob would answer. Her words echoed through his mind—let it ring let it ring let it ring—and he remembered how, when he answered in defiance of her, he felt bad, but also kind of good. It felt bad, but also kind of good, that she hated him like she hated his dad.

He remembered when he had to go to court. Had to dress up like it was church. The judge had looked at him and asked the question once, and then again when Bob didn't answer right away.

"Would you rather live with your mother or your father?"

"My dad," he'd said.

Lots of people were entering his hospital room.

His fevered eyes studied them. They weren't nurses or orderlies or other patients; the colors of their outfits interrupted the pastel everything. Bob blinked and the room spun and refocused. They were young people, high schoolers maybe, maybe on a class trip.

And then he recognized Lisa. He knew Lisa from school; she was one of the two girls in the world he'd ever kissed. They'd been fifteen, walking down a street in town. When she put her lips on his, a street preacher on a platform pointed and said, "Repent, you sinner, and come to Christ!" and Bob wondered why he was being called a sinner.

He hadn't worked up the nerve to kiss Lisa again that day.

What was she doing at the hospital?

Bob tried to sit up but his body was a sack of hot rocks.

He was sure he had once known a girl named Lisa and he was sure that he saw her now.

"Lisa!" Bob screamed at the line of kids.

She looked startled and turned.

She walked towards him and asked, "What are you doing here?"

"My dad put me here," he said, surprised at how hard it was to form words.

"Why did he do that?" she asked. He could see in her eyes how bad he looked. He could see her not wanting to linger.

70

"I don't know," he managed.

"Goodbye, Bob," she said.

She was gone.

He never would figure out why she was there.

For weeks, maybe, he remained like this, SMELLING MY OWN SICKNESS and watching THE STREET OUTSIDE ENDLESSLY THROUGH THE CAGED WINDOW:

Late one stormy night through bullets of rain, he saw a figure and two large dogs on leashes, German shepherds like police have, walking slowly down the street. The figure turned and walked back. It repeated this for hours. Bob wondered what it was all about.

That was until he fell into ACOMA.

A Blank

Gene did not recall much about the early years when he sought mental health care for his son. It was a topic that he certainly didn't seem comfortable being asked about. He couldn't remember the first time he took Bob to Herrick Hospital specifically, nor what events led him to do so. But he was skeptical of Bob's account. He never hosted a graduation party, let alone one at which he'd made Bob feel unwelcome. When he occasionally had students over for beer or coffee, Bob was always free to join: "He was never offensive or embarrassing," Gene said. His ex-girlfriend Pat would have had nothing to do with Bob being hospitalized. Nobody would ever call a hospital a "really fun place," he said.

Bob always went into the hospital, he said, "as a result of some incident."

I asked again if he remembered what incident preceded Bob's first hospitalization.

"I don't," he said. "It could have been something at school. There was another time he was driving around with a knife on the seat of the car and frightened some girls."

He didn't recall the other psychiatrist Bob described, the one whose office was on Shattuck Avenue. He said it was possible such a man existed. Maybe he'd been a regular physician who'd made the psychiatric referral, though Gene's best guess was that Herrick had been referred to him by a colleague.

But Gene couldn't, or wouldn't, name the incident that had

occurred, or the behavior he'd observed, that had caused him to take Bob to Herrick Hospital.

"There has to have been something," he said. "I'm just drawing a blank, Sandy."

He offered one memory that might have had something to do with it. He and Bob were playing tennis; it must have been at the Claremont Hotel. Rather than play, Bob was just standing there, grinning. "I couldn't awaken him, really," Gene said. "He was just standing there on the court with a big smile on his face. I could have taken him then."

Gene said he always attributed what happened to Bob to a promise he'd made—and broken—during the divorce. He had told Bob that he wasn't going to have to go to court. Then, because of something Marilyn did, it turned out Bob had to go and talk to the judge.

"He was never quite the same after that," Gene said. He couldn't say how. "Withdrawn," he said. "I don't know. Different. Things were very difficult then. It's hard for me to think back."

Other details Bob described about his time at Herrick Hospital, like getting German measles or falling into a coma, also didn't sound real to Gene. He remembered visiting Bob at Herrick, watching a movie. Another time he was there and Bob had just gotten a spinal tap or something. He guessed it must have been diagnostic.

Bob was lying in a bed. He looked so "pathetic."

That day, Gene said, he nearly cried.

I asked if he blamed anyone or anything for what happened to Bob—Marilyn, for example, or the drugs. Gene said all the arguing probably didn't help anything, but he didn't blame her.

As for the drugs, he said that Bob became candid about his drug use many years later. He said Bob himself had speculated that the drugs had been responsible.

I asked Gene if he thought, therefore, that what happened to Bob was Bob's own fault.

"I never thought in terms of fault," he said, "I thought in terms of tragedy."

::WEEEEE:::

A brain doesn't just turn back on after a coma—it swings on and off—so the memories he kept were small. His dad was there, and Pat, and a friend of theirs. Pat had flowers. His dad tried to touch him and Bob felt a searing evil and passed out again.

He remembered, when he was awake for good this time, how stale his mouth tasted, and when he tried to talk, how his saliva felt like a creek running with a winter's first rain. He was in intensive care, they told him, in a hospital in San Francisco.

He remembered this one nurse, maybe the guy was gay, pointing at Bob's skinny stomach, at his ribs, and saying, "Sophia Loren!"

They were always feeding him ham sandwiches. He puked the first time he ate one, puked all down the side of his tall hospital bed and the sheets and blankets. The memory of puke lingered in the room after.

One day three nurses set him in a wheelchair and pushed him down a hallway into a little room. His knees were like match heads. They put big headphones on him that pinched his brow.

"Tell me when the beeps match," the guy said, and Bob puked into a trash can.

Then came the spinal tap. Nobody bothered to tell him what it was or why he needed it but it hurt, hurt worse than maybe anything he'd ever felt.

When he woke, he was back in his bed. A nurse apologized later, said they'd messed up the spinal tap and they were going to have to do another, which they then did, and it hurt the same again.

In time his brain started to hum again. Soon he ate maybe two or three ham sandwiches a day. He liked them a lot. Just ham and a little bit of butter on white bread.

His dad showed up with his brother, Bob's uncle, and a pair of Bob's jeans, and a shirt. They stood facing the window while Bob slowly dressed. A nurse helped him into a wheelchair.

They all got in his dad's Cadillac and drove across the City and onto the Bay Bridge. Bob set his head against the glass and looked down at the brackish water far below. Everything made him a little dizzy. He closed his eyes. The car was quiet; his father and uncle were not talkative men. And the trenches that had existed before between Bob and his dad were now deep enough you couldn't see the bottom. Last his dad had seen Bob, really, was that day he dropped him at Herrick. The version of his son he'd collected now was twenty pounds lighter, and furious. He'd been through things that nobody, really, would ever understand.

The only thing Bob remembered his dad saying

during that drive home from the hospital was,
:::THOSE HAM SANDWICHES COST ME A FORTUNE::

Back at his dad's condo, Bob spent his days hanging around while Merna, the maid, cooked and cleaned. He still didn't like to eat what she made. He didn't trust her because there was no real way to prove she wasn't going to poison him. Why bother risking his life just to feel sated? Bob sat on the sofa maybe playing guitar, maybe talking about what had happened to him at Herrick Hospital—about that devil asshole Dr. G. and the orderlies and nurses and everybody else. They're calling *him* sick; *they're* the ones who are sick. If his dad walked in from work and saw an untouched sandwich on the table, or heard Bob talking about such things, he'd yell that he worked damn hard to afford all this. He'd yell that Bob got the best medical care money could buy.

His dad had hired a tutor for Bob who'd come by sometimes. Who knows how much his dad was paying for the guy but Jesus if his dad had actually hung out and saw what a waste it all was. The tutor assigned a book report and Bob copied a passage about war out of the encyclopedia and the guy gave him an A. After the tutor left that day, Bob fell back onto the sofa laughing.

It was all such a joke.

Fortune for a fucking ham sandwich his ass.

He thought about last summer, and the one before that, when he'd gone on these long hiking trips with a bunch of guys down in the Sierras. They were his dad's idea, these trips; perhaps, Bob figured, his dad wanted to be rid of Bob so he could hang out with his girlfriends.

Bob remembered flying down to Los Angeles that first year. He'd been fifteen.

At the airport he met a few of the guys. Bud, who was in charge, and PIUTE, AN INDIAN WHO I TOOK AN EMEDIATE LIKING TO:

They got in the cab of a truck and drove several hours east to a town called Independence.

The outfit had fourteen guys in total, and forty donkeys. Each boy was responsible for a few. Bob had EGOR, TAGALONG, ANDANOTHERICANT RE MEMBER HIS NAME:

They packed their donkeys, hoisted on their unfamiliar, heavy packs, and began their first ascent.

After a few hours, they pitched their first camp, and spent the afternoon learning safety skills on a nearby glacier.

That night, Bob got in his sleeping bag.

It was odd to lie on something so hard and so cold, but he was so exhausted he drifted off.

Someone's hand was on his shoulder.

Bob blinked awake.

It was Piute.

"Get up," Piute said.

It was dark out still. Piute moved on to another tent. Bob wriggled out of his sleeping bag into the greater cold. His hands smelled like fire and his jeans were stiff.

The other guys, he saw, were following Bud up a ridge. He hastened to join them. Behind the mountains, a fringe of rose-colored sun betrayed itself. Bud commanded them to stop. Beneath, the black lake slept.

Each guy looked to his neighbor, wondering what was going on.

"All in," Bud yelled.

No one moved.

"You heard what I said, everybody in," he said. Bob could make out Piute's grin.

The guys moaned. Bob felt the hair on his arms battered by the breeze.

A few guys around him started unlacing their boots. Bob heard the first splash and commotion and whooping. Another splash. Another. Bob didn't want to embarrass himself, so he undressed, fast, and he leapt.

He hung in the dark air for what felt like a very long time before—oh—that shock of water and he was a tiny warm thing in it, naked as a trout.

Each morning, they listened for the donkeys' bells across the high dry earth. They wrangled, packed them, and packed out.

Each day, they'd cover twenty or thirty miles. It was hard work, but it was invigorating. Bob could feel himself growing stronger. Once, Bob watched nauseated as the guys flipped some donkeys onto their backs and castrated them—shocks of blood on the brown earth.

Each evening, they'd set up a camp and sit around the fire, telling each other stories and laughing about shit.

One night, there was a huge storm and lightning nearly struck Bob's tent. Another, they camped on what turned out to be a scorpion den. Bob awoke with a bag of shiny sharp bugs, screaming. Piute came running and gave him a shot of something. Piute had saved his life.

A few weeks in, they returned to Independence for supplies.

Some of them went to a diner in town and ordered burgers. There were some girls at the counter with shakes. One of Bob's friends turned to him and said, "Go ask them."

"For what?" Bob asked.

"To give you a blowjob, man!" The other guys were cracking up. They'd been talking about blowjobs for days. Bob didn't really get what it meant, but he wanted to keep making the other guys crack up. He stood and walked over to the girls, who went silent. He looked like a mountain man, a mountain man with long golden hair.

"Hi," Bob said.

"Hi," one of the girls said, the one in the middle.

"I was wondering if you'd give me a blowjob?" he said.

The girls looked all shocked and giggled. After a moment the one in the middle—she was unreal—said, "Sure."

The girl hopped off her stool and went out back. He stayed quiet, just followed her calves. A dumpster stank. She set her little fingers on the top of his jeans. Beneath his flannel Bob felt sweat trickling down his sides. There was dust in her brown hair.

Bob didn't love her. Bob didn't even know her.

"I'm sorry," he stammered, backing away.

He went back inside and bought a Coke.

Out front, Bruce, Piute, and Bob started walking down the road towards their group's equipment shack, joining some of the rest of their crew. A few guys, must have been locals, were walking about twenty feet behind them.

Bob glanced back and saw more local guys were joining.

They were nearly to the equipment shack now and the gang of locals had swelled to about thirteen.

Then someone hit his friend Tom in the head with a rock and everything was a blur.

Bob and some others sprinted into the shack and grabbed what he could. One guy had a MASHETI:

Guys were wailing on each other.

It was his FIRST GANG WAR.

Eventually the locals took off.

Consensus amongst Bob and his crew was they had won.

Bob was glad.

He was more glad, after, to return to the mountains.

Before they left Independence, they all went to some house. They sat around a television and watched as a man, an American, landed for the first time on the moon.

Bob learned to bake bread in a stone cooker and wash clothes by a fire. On rest days, Piute was teaching him how to climb mountains. They'd pack some cheese and an oatmeal ball and an orange and head out. Bob liked just scaling up a mountain however he could, and having no fear.

On the top of a peak would usually be a metal box with a slip of paper and pencil inside where other people who'd made it would have written their name and the date. In one box the last signature was from 1890.

Beneath it, Bob signed his.

His dad had given him a small Instamatic camera that could take seventy-two half-frame shots a roll. He took pictures of everything he saw. Shedding cliffs. Stands of spear-like trees. Little alpine lakes the shape of tears. Though Piute was annoyed that Bob was constantly stopping to photograph something, Bob did not regret how many pictures he took.

One time Bob asked Piute whether he'd be back next year.

"Probably not," Piute said.

"Why not, man?"

"Probably be drafted by then."

They hiked in silence for a while after that.

It was a sad day when Bob said farewell to his donkeys and watched as they wandered back off into the desert. He said goodbye to some of the guys and got back in the van and left Independence.

Back in Berkeley, his friends bragged about their summers—the parties they'd gone to, the concerts they'd seen, the girls they'd had. They were passing around a joint. One of his buddies had fucked some Catholic chick in a boat.

"I felt like a fucking god!" he said, smoke coming out of his nose like a cartoon bull.

Bob didn't even KNOW HOW TO MASTERBATE:

The next summer, Bob had returned to the
Sierras, to the same two-month excursion. He
could tell right away, though, that things were
different. Piute wasn't there. Bob wondered if
he'd been drafted but nobody seemed to know.
The leader was now some millionaire in his
sixties. Everything was a mess. One kid broke
his leg. Another wandered off for days. All the
days of hikes and the donkeys blurred into one
memory with the first summer. Bob spent a lot
of time cooking. And he snuck off to smoke weed
whenever he could; he'd smuggled a jar this
time in his duffel.

On the flight back from L.A., he got a terrible
headache. He sat next to a chick on the plane
who asked if she could have a ride from the
airport. His dad drove up in a Buick Electra
Convertible and grudgingly agreed. They dropped
her off, Bob's head still throbbing.

He saw his friends soon after and it was
the same as before. They told Bob about all
the cool shit they'd done—the parties and the
girls—and he felt even more left behind.

Now, sitting on his ass at his dad's condo,
thin and sick and on the other side of having
not died, Bob laughed at how weak his arms
looked and felt. He couldn't imagine trying
to carry a pack, or hiking twenty miles, or
climbing a peak.

Maybe it was for the best that none of his
friends seemed to remember he existed.

If he had seen anybody they'd have had
questions, besides.

Why had he been kicked out of high school?

Where had he been since?

Why had he been at Herrick Hospital in the first place—what would he say if they asked him that?

One day his dad explained that he had to go to Singapore, to teach a semester there. He told Bob he could either come along or stay behind and go to a boarding school across the bay in Marin County. There'd be wild monkeys in Singapore, his dad said, but it was a strict country: Bob would have to cut his hair, and go to military school.

Bob didn't much like the sound of that, and chose to go to the school in Marin, which was called Sunny Hills. They had to drive by San Quentin prison to get there. Bob looked at the prison's thin windows, where men inside waited to die either from time or an electric chair.

Sunny Hills, it turned out, was too happy a name for what this place actually was. Yes, there were hills, dry ones pocked with big green oaks, and yes, it was often sunny, as a big mountain mostly shielded their valley from the nightly fog. It wasn't like a normal school or anything; it was more like a camp—just a few wooden buildings, some used as classrooms, some as dorms.

He had a dog, a scruffy black thing he called Wendy. Merna the maid had given it to him.

The other kids at Sunny Hills were all messed up. Some of them had done time or just flunked out real hard. Some of them were mean like a dog who'd been kicked in the head. You didn't always know what was wrong with everyone, and Bob didn't care to find out. He stayed away from them and they stayed away from him. They didn't like his dog, besides.

He would walk Wendy after dinner, when the sun was setting and he didn't need to worry about getting sunburned. An old lady cooked all their meals, and he was finally gaining back some weight. He had found a graveyard up there. He was sure nobody else at the school even realized it existed.

The dusk lingered.

Bob liked it up there, alone. It reminded him, somewhat, of being up in the Sierras, last summer and the one before.

Ravens stood in the oak ahead.

"Caw," he said to them.

"Caw, caw."

Wendy scampered through the blond grasses between the graves.

One time she'd run right up to a skunk. Much to Bob's disbelief, the skunk hadn't sprayed her but had turned around and walked away.

A few months into his time at Sunny Hills, there'd been a parents' day.

His dad hadn't come all the way from Singapore, obviously, and his mom didn't show either.

Bob sat around, watched all the other kids with their parents.

They did let him and two other kids play some music that day. Bob had his guitar, another guy had a little drum kit. They didn't sound half bad.

::::::

The only person who'd come to visit him was this kid Tony. Tony's family used to live near his mom's. As kids, Bob and Tony used to ride their bikes around the hills, or go mess around at the Claremont Hotel. One time they'd gone into the City and bought fireworks in Chinatown that they'd later set off in Tony's backyard.

Bob didn't know how Tony had heard Bob was at Sunny Hills, but he must have called and gotten permission to take him out. Bob was impressed when Tony showed up in a VW Beetle so new it still had paper plates.

They drove south on 101, across the Golden Gate into the City. They ended up in North Beach, at a strip club, where a woman without a top on rubbed up and down on some pole.

They were only sixteen but the lady had served them anyway. Bob slurped his drink. Tony was talking about heading to college.

"And what are you thinking of doing next?" Tony asked.

Bob paused. Looked at his drink.

"I don't know, man," he answered.

After, they tried to buy some dirty magazines from a vendor on the street, but he wanted an ID. Up and down Broadway the clubs' marquees seized and shone and big dudes stood out front moving velvet ropes and cabs spat out schools of sailors and out-of-towners, and the arriving night fog made Bob's skin prick. They got back in the VW.

The fog glowed orange around the lights on the bridge.

After they arrived at Sunny Hills, the guard let Bob in; Tony drove away.

Bob felt relief when he got to his little dorm bed and heard Wendy's tail thumping on the sheets.

Since Tony's visit, he'd become consumed with the dread that his life was going to mean nothing. His peers at Sunny Hills were such losers. Bob hated feeling like them. He kept asking his teacher if there was a test he could take to get high school over with. They handed him a book and he drew a map of Egypt and Iran.

I WAS GETTING KIND OF WEORD:

Since Tony's visit, he had only gotten to leave Sunny Hills two other times. One was when they loaded them all onto buses and drove them over to Berkeley to see the Nitty Gritty Dirt Band.

Bob hadn't realized they'd be seeing a show on Berkeley High's campus. He got real nervous as he walked inside.

He saw someone he knew from high school, a kid named Matt.

"Hey!" Matt said, and Bob said hey back, his pulse rising. The room was so large, and there were so many people in it. The band hadn't even begun to play but Bob couldn't take it. He asked a teacher for permission to go back to the bus.

The driver let him on, and he stretched out across the seat in back, half-listening to the show's muffled sound.

The other time he'd gotten to leave Sunny Hills was just after Christmas. His dad was back from

Singapore and picked Bob up. They drove to Tahoe. In a few days, Bob would be seventeen.

On his birthday morning, he awoke in the cold bedroom downstairs and walked up to the living room. Through the drapes Lake Tahoe was huge and icy blue. Bob peeled the paper off his present's box. It was a Johnny Race Car set, a toy for five-year-olds.

His dad snapped the track together. He put one of the cars at the top of the track and let it go.

::WEEEEE::: his dad said, grinning into Bob's face.

I GUESS THE GUY THOUGHT I WAS A RETARD AND I HATED HIM FOR IT:

His dad had DUMPED him back at Sunny Hills two nights ago and returned to Singapore. When Bob got to his room, he opened the closet and discovered something unimaginably bad: someone had stolen his guitar!

He went BALLISTIC.

At group meeting he had looked at each and every one of the kids and called them what they were: crooks.

Later, at the dorm, he made THRETENING BODY SIGNALLS TO A COUPLLE KIDS IN MY DO RM LIKE ID KILL THEM WITH MY KNIOFE:

He walked up to the graveyard.

He needed to cool down.

He sat on a rock and wondered who had that kind of nerve to steal something so important from him.

He could hear the hum of Highway 101.

In the sky, he could make out some stars.

He looked down at his dog, who sat patiently by.

He looked again at the sky. Something had caught his eye.

An airplane?

He looked and—there!—he saw it again.

He couldn't tell what it was, but it was moving.

He kept staring, trying to decide whether his eyes were playing tricks on him, but the more he focused on it, the more he was certain there was something there, something blocking out just the stars at first, and then a stand of clouds, SOME DARK SHADOW OF SOME CRAFT:

It was coming closer.

Couldn't be an airplane.

Bob squinted and as he did a ray of energy hit him in the head, throwing him onto the dust.

He blacked out.

His tongue was on the ground and his arms splayed wide.

He rose.

What just happened?

What the fuck just happened?

His mind whirred.

Dust on his jeans and gravel in his palms and dirt in his mouth. He started running back down toward the school. Something incredible had just happened to him. Wendy scampered to keep up.

His legs and his mind raced. All his life, he'd been like a donkey, like a donkey corralled and thrown upside down and castrated by an Indian. Or he'd been like an Indian, an Indian whose skull had probably been punctured by a Vietcong bullet by now. All those fuckers like that old shrink on Shattuck and Dr. G. and the nurses and orderlies at Herrick and that tutor and Merna the maid and the crooks here at Sunny Hills, and his dad putting that little car on the track and grinning "Weeeee"—all of them with their clicking pens and quiet judgment, all of them did not get it. There was something in the sky. This was the best moment of Bob's life so far. This was when he realized that, no matter what, there was something bigger than all of this. There was an energy ray in the heavens and it had elected to come down and touch him.

He was back at his dorm now. Weirdly, there were five chicks hanging out in the common room but no guys. He went to his room but something was wrong with the door. He had his key but it wasn't working. He shook the knob a bit, and tried again. Nothing. He tried again.

He backed up and prepared to kick it, muttering, "What the fuck is wrong with this fucking goddamn door," when some girl opened it from the inside.

"What are you doing here?" he said. She was confusing him, being inside his room.

Only later did he understand it wasn't his. He hadn't realized there were two dorms that looked exactly alike. An honest mistake. During his conversation with the counselor who had rushed to the scene, he also mentioned the energy ray that had reached down from the heavens. That was also a mistake.

::::

They woke him before dawn with their hands and their needles. He tried to protest.

They lowered him into a car.

The Richmond-San Rafael Bridge's towers blinked red in the gray predawn. Speeding back to Herrick Hospital, Bob looked behind to San Quentin, where, awaiting their deaths, the prisoners were still asleep.

You Can Call It Anything

I have often looked back and tried to remember what I thought the word "schizophrenia" meant before Bob sent his manuscript to me. I've asked myself what images flashed through my mind when I first read the phrase he typed on his manuscript's cover page: `psychotic paranoid schizophrenic`.

I'd note that he took care to spell the entire phrase correctly there. And that he didn't use the word for the diagnosis itself, "schizophrenia," but rather for what that diagnosis supposedly made him, "schizophrenic." Other than this prominent instance, words like "schizophrenia" or "schizophrenic" or "schizoid" appear in Bob's manuscript very rarely. When they do, it's often in scenes when he needed a word to explain himself to somebody else, often somebody with a badge and a gun.

The short answer is I didn't know what it meant. What ideas I had were fuzzy and ugly; they'd maybe come from movies, or from the news. I can't remember whether I'd known that was his diagnosis before he sent me his manuscript; perhaps I'd heard my mother mutter it before.

I tried to figure out the answer in books. The more books I read, though, the more it became clear that there was no simple answer as to what schizophrenia is, or what causes it. There was, if anything, a charged and polarized disagreement, a complicated one, one I had never known about before.

So I started talking with people who knew more than I did about what the word "schizophrenia" might mean. Some had been diagnosed with it, others had relatives who'd been diagnosed. I spoke with psychiatrists who'd given the diagnosis, and psychologists and social workers and others who worked with people who'd received it. I spoke with academics, as well as researchers who study schizophrenia, including geneticists who are searching for signs of it inside the body somewhere.

Because, I'd learned right away, a psychiatric diagnosis like schizophrenia is a hypothesis. There is no test to prove you have schizophrenia. The best doctor on earth cannot "see" schizophrenia in your blood, in your hair, in your piss, in your genes.

The word itself was coined in 1908, by a famous Swiss psychiatrist. He was part of a wave of psychiatrists who sought to scientifically classify diseases of the mind, which, frustratingly, remained mysterious and incurable, even as there were spectacular advances in other medical fields. Unable to see inside patients' brains, these psychiatrists would instead make long-term observations of populations of asylum patients, or study psychiatric records, and then extrapolate distinct hypothetical diseases from clusters of symptoms and their progressions. They favored Greek- and Latinate-sounding terms, ones they sometimes embedded with metaphor that implied something about the disorder in question. Etymologically, the word "psychiatrist" itself means "soul doctor."

Thinking of "madness"—as it has been and sometimes still is called—as literal disease is pretty new in the scheme of human history, yet this view is by no means ubiquitous worldwide today. In the West, this idea arose during industrialization, as did professionalized psychiatry. Before then, the consensus in much of Europe and America had been that "mad people" were possessed by the devil. They were often tortured accordingly. Throughout the history of psychiatry, successive generations have considered themselves fortunate to have advanced past the barbaric ways of yesteryear.

"Schizophrenia" existed first as a plural. It was *die Schizophrenie* in the original, or "the schizophrenias." Etymologically, its halves are usually translated to mean "split" or "cleave" and "brain." This split-brain metaphor has no basis when it comes to the structure or function of the brains of people diagnosed with schizophrenia, or at least none that's ever been found. "Schizophrenia" was invented to replace another diagnosis, "dementia praecox," or "premature dementia." "Dementia Praecox" had been coined only a few decades prior by a famous German psychiatrist. For some decades both "schizophrenia" and "dementia praecox" were in use. Psychiatrists disagreed about whether these diagnoses were synonyms, or distinct disorders, or whether one was a subcategory of the other. Eventually "dementia praecox" fell out of use and "schizophrenia" stuck around.

By the mid–twentieth century, some American psychiatrists grew frustrated with the lack of standardized diagnoses. In 1952, the American Psychiatric Association, or APA, published the first edition of the *Diagnostic and Statistical Manual of Mental Disorders,* or *DSM*, which is sometimes called psychiatry's "Bible."

By the time Bob was hospitalized in about 1970, many American psychiatrists were favoring the use of the *DSM* to guide the diagnosis—and therefore treatment—of "mental patients," as they had come to be called. The *DSM* was then on its second edition. It defined "schizophrenia" as a "large category" of disorders "manifested by characteristic disturbances of thinking, mood and behavior." It described how patients with schizophrenia often had disturbed thinking that would lead to "misinterpretation of reality and sometimes to delusions and hallucinations, which frequently appear psychologically self-protective." The subdiagnosis of "paranoid schizophrenia" was "characterized primarily by the presence of persecutory or grandiose delusions, often associated with hallucinations. Excessive religiosity is sometimes seen. The patient's attitude is frequently hostile and aggressive, and his behavior tends to be consistent with his delusions."

Bob would have been about sixteen when he was diagnosed. In this respect and others, his is what psychiatrists might regard as a textbook case of schizophrenia. Boys are often diagnosed during the teenage years; for girls, diagnosis tends to come a bit later. Like Bob, individuals diagnosed with schizophrenia will frequently have their first struggles in social situations and in school; as a result some believe symptoms actually begin earlier, during puberty. Diagnosis often follows an acute event of some kind, like an episode of what psychiatrists call "psychosis."

For decades, researchers have sought to answer basic questions about schizophrenia: What is it? What causes it? Numerous environmental factors have been scrutinized for their potential role. Some factors, like being born in winter, having an older father, or a mother having experienced illness during pregnancy have been shown to relate to a higher instance of schizophrenia diagnosis. Research has found that schizophrenia seems to run in some families. It's also been found that someone with an identical twin who's been diagnosed isn't necessarily going to be diagnosed as well, but is likelier to.

One of the most studied ideas as to what causes schizophrenia is the "chemical imbalance theory," which derives psychiatric pharmaceuticals themselves. Though the "mechanism of action" of drugs marketed for their "antipsychotic" properties isn't understood—plainly, drug companies believe these drugs are effective in lessening psychiatric symptoms, but they don't actually know why—what is known is that they affect chemical levels in the brain. It's therefore supposed that abnormal chemical levels might somehow be crucial to understanding what's different about the brains of people diagnosed with schizophrenia. Testing chemical levels inside brains remains impossible. Despite billions of dollars of investigation, the chemical imbalance theory has never been confirmed.

Since Bob was diagnosed, the definition of schizophrenia put forth by the *DSM* has continued to shift. When the third edition was released in 1980, other diagnoses were separated out from schizophrenia, most notably autism. Subtypes like "paranoid schizophrenia" were later done away with because of the lack of clear evidence for what distinguished them from one another.

Since he was diagnosed, some theories as to what causes schizophrenia have been largely abandoned. For example, a popular idea from the 1960s was that the disorder was caused by "schizophrenogenic parents"—usually "schizophrenogenic mothers"—whose emotional behavior caused their child's brain disease. Parents who were led to blame themselves for their children's illnesses went on to found the largest support group for relatives and other caregivers of people diagnosed with mental illnesses, the National Alliance on Mental Illness, or NAMI.

Some people feel that no amount of research will ever yield answers to basic questions about schizophrenia because the word "schizophrenia" doesn't refer to any actual disease. They argue that psychiatric diagnoses only reflect the biases of those giving them, whether individual or social. They point to antique diagnoses that, in hindsight, betray this phenomenon extremely. There was "Drapetomania", for example, a now-abandoned hypothetical illness from the mid–nineteenth century that described a slave who sought freedom. These critics may point to other qualities that were once pathologized but are no longer, like left-handedness or homosexuality. Some fault our "ableist" or "sanist" dominant culture. Some charge that we too easily believe that science can explain all things, even things that remain fundamentally mysterious, like the human mind. Or that we too eagerly believe in an imaginary standard called "normal."

Many people who feel this way have themselves at some point been diagnosed with schizophrenia. Many dispute their diagnoses. Many, as Bob did on his manuscript's cover page, call the diagnosis itself a "label," a tool used to discriminate against, confine, discredit, and silence. Like Bob, many people who come to feel this way have had experiences in psychiatric settings that were unhelpful or even traumatic.

Some who've been told by doctors that they have schizophrenia or are schizophrenic argue that receiving such a diagnosis is itself damaging, given, for example, how many negative stereotypes there are about what such words mean. Diagnosis itself is a "social death," one self-identified "psychiatric survivor" told me: "Being called and labeled with certain names and epithets can truly have the power to deeply scar or even destroy a person's sense of self," he described. The event of being diagnosed erodes an individual's sense of self-worth and can lead to "a life of self-fulfilling prophesy of despair and giving up."

Many feel that those seeking to help individuals perceived to be abnormal or experiencing mental or emotional distress shouldn't seek to diagnose them, to call some of their behaviors or experiences "symptoms" and try to fit them into one box or another. Rather, those seeking to provide mental health care should work to better understand the various contexts in which people actually live—for example, the deleterious effects of poverty, racism, sexism, bullying, and other traumas.

In recent years especially, some mental health care professionals have joined in critiquing the "medical model" of psychiatric illness, as it's sometimes shorthanded, the belief that psychiatric illnesses are illnesses like any other and are best treated with medications. Some psychologists have drifted in this direction, as well as a few psychiatrists, mostly in Europe, who sometimes call themselves "social psychiatrists." Some psychologists and psychiatrists focus their work on people who seem to be in their own reality; they contend that such people can be reached, and helped. I asked one such dissident social psychiatrist what he made of his mainstream colleagues and their fidelity to a guidebook and set of ideas that to him are arcane and cruel. He called them "priests" of a religion.

Many professionals who work with people who've been diagnosed with schizrenia, especially psychiatrists, regard such points of view as gravely misguided. Many people I spoke with expressed certainty that schizophrenia is a real disease, albeit one that is not yet understood biologically. Today, it's widely held that the answers to what schizophrenia is or what causes it will come from further genetic study. Some evidence suggests "schizophrenia" may refer to several distinct conditions, genetically speaking.

"It is a very real disease," one geneticist said to me, displeased, it seemed, that I'd even asked such a bizarre question. The schizophrenia researchers I interviewed tended to be unfamiliar with the controversy regarding the category itself. The psychiatrists I spoke with, however, seemed very aware of these debates and were often eager to rebut them. Some likened those who criticize psychiatry or psychiatric drugs to those who speciously question the clear efficacy of vaccines, for example. Some psychiatrists dismissed their critics on the grounds that they are crazy.

People who told me they know schizophrenia is real explained that they've seen it in their clinics, or their private offices. Or they've seen it in their own families. And some who have been diagnosed with schizophrenia agree that that's what they have. Many professionals I spoke with said that a precise diagnosis is crucial in determining the best course of treatment. Many said that the medications available today to treat schizophrenia are by no means perfect but they are the best solution we have. They explained that finding the right dose of the right medication can take time and patience and that patients often need additional support—therapy, for example. Many feel that questioning the meaning of "schizophrenia" or the efficacy of these medications only encourages people who might already be "treatment resistant" to eschew the help they seriously need.

This is risky, many feel, because of the nature of this disease. A prominent psychiatrist explained to me that schizophrenia is a developmental disorder that affects our most recently evolved brain systems. It affects thinking, causing disordered or paranoid processing that may crystallize into delusions. It affects perception, in extreme cases causing hallucination and psychosis.

It affects cognitive abilities—the ability to remember, to make judgments, to analyze information, to be creative—as well as emotions. Some people diagnosed with schizophrenia also exhibit physical or verbal tics more often associated with autism or Tourette's. He additionally described the disorder as degenerative, over time slowly robbing an individual of her personality, as well as her ability to function. "People become zombie-like," he said. He, like many professionals and family of people diagnosed with schizophrenia, lamented how stigmatized the word itself has become.

In recent decades, a few countries' psychiatric associations have therefore swapped out their term for "schizophrenia" with a new one that doesn't evoke a head cracked in half. In Japan, the diagnosis now roughly translates to "integration disorder." In South Korea, their new word for "schizophrenia" is one that evokes an image about wind chimes, an expression in Korean that comes from a sixteenth-century monk: "As a stringed instrument maintains its own sounds with appropriate tension, the human mind also needs adequate tuning to maintain its functions." Supporters of this term say it better implies the notion that the disorder has something to do with neural circuitry. Some psychiatrists argue that this term should be replaced with something more akin to the autism spectrum, for example a "Psychosis Spectrum Syndrome."

I asked schizophrenia researchers whether they thought something like marijuana or LSD could cause schizophrenia, something I'd wondered when I first read Bob's manuscript. Several answered that hallucinogens could potentially hasten onset for someone who already has a genetic proclivity, but they were each careful to say that no one knows for sure what causes it. They said it doesn't seem likely that we will ever find a single surefire environmental trigger, nor a single responsible gene; that in fact, genetically, it seems likelier that numerous genes working together result in schizophrenia. It isn't a solo but a symphony. But they emphasized that much remains unknown, and until schizophrenia is better understood, therapies that are actually responsive to any underlying disorder—rather than, at best, dulling some symptoms—will remain a fantasy. One geneticist remarked to me that "of course" the medications available today "aren't very good. They're technology from the fifties," she said.

Gene didn't remember when he first heard his son's diagnosis, nor from whom. I asked what he remembered learning about it back then, what he remembered reading. He explained that because it wasn't his field, his inclination was to trust his son's doctors rather than read "from scratch out of books." He recalled understanding that the disorder had something to do with imbalanced chemical levels in the brain.

"A diagnosis like that is all a little bit woozy," he went on, explaining he'd certainly heard the term "paranoid schizo," and certainly you can see the paranoia, and you can see the disturbed mind, particularly when he's off medication—the hearing voices and seeing angels come down and things like that."

Gene also referred to the diagnosis itself as a "label."

"It never really mattered to me what you call it," he said, "You can call it anything, just so long as you're getting the right treatment."

A LIVING
ZOMBIE:

IT STARTED OUT BAD, like before, being injected with drugs, being thrown into seclusion a couple of times. HELL, one night they even handcuffed him to the bed.

He yanked and jerked but couldn't break free. All he could move was his head. He could see that the guy in the bed next to him was shackled, too. Some orderlies came in and shot the guy full of something and an hour later, Bob watched the rise and fall of the guy's chest stop altogether.

In the morning, the orderlies came in and put a sheet over the corpse. As they wheeled it away, Bob could hear them laughing.

Another night, Bob peered through his dark room. There was a light coming from another room across the hall and something was moving. Bob wondered for a moment what it was and then realized it was a head, a woman's head, a woman's head dipping up and down. Bob couldn't see her face because of her hair, but he could see the grinning face of the orderly seated with his cock in her mouth. There was another person in the room with them—Bob could make out now—another orderly, and he was injecting a needle into his arm and grinning.

Bob again watched the girl giving the first guy head. THE GUY FLOATED AROUND EMENSLY HAPPY WHEN HE CAME:

Bob had done a lot of thinking about what had happened to him at Sunny Hills. The questions the doctors and nurses had asked made it clear that nobody believed him. They were waiting for the day that he would take it back, when he'd say, oh never mind, I *didn't* get selected by the universe to understand its true nature.

He realized he had a choice: he could either lie to them and wait to turn eighteen, which was when he understood they couldn't hold him any longer, or he could maintain what he knew to be true and stay there for who knows how long and have his stay at Herrick on his adult record. When he was talking with the hospital staff or sharing something during group, he downplayed his new beliefs. Privately, though, those beliefs grew.

He didn't know what the energy beam had actually been—aliens or what. What it was didn't much matter. Because of it, Bob for the first time felt the relief of realizing the littleness of humanity compared with the vast unknown. And yet he was stuck there, and awful things were happening—guys were dying in the night, and orderlies were laughing about it. Orderlies were getting head, and others shooting up. Who could he tell about what was going on?

He couldn't tell Dr. G., who always said he'd cut back the meds but then lied. Dr. G. who'd appear on the floor only when a new female patient was admitted. He'd spend a long time alone with her, emerging WITH A HARDON AND A SMILE: Bob worried if he tried to tell anybody about what he'd seen, he'd be the next body they wheeled away at dawn.

Then Bob got a great idea: he could ask to see a priest. That, he knew, they couldn't refuse. Next time he saw Dr. G. he said, "I'd like to see a priest."

"Why would you like that?" Dr. G. asked.

"I want to talk about God," Bob said, adding, "I'm into that, man."

A few days later Dr. G. led in the priest and then stood outside the room.

"I don't want him hearing what we say," Bob told the priest, nodding to the door.

"It's just you and me," said the priest.

"He's standing right there—"

"Do you know Christ, son?" asked the priest.

"I don't want *him* knowing if I do."

"Do you have a relationship with Christ?"

"They're killing people in here, man—" Bob figured he wouldn't have long before Dr. G. came back.

"Christ loves you, son."

"You're not listening, man, the guy in the bed next to me a few weeks ago, they let him die, they were laughing, man. I saw it—"

An orderly and Dr. G. came back in the room. The priest left and they pressed Bob against the floor and little bits of dirt from other people's shoes were on his cheek.

Next the universe sent someone to protect him.

One day, about four months into this second stay at Herrick Hospital, Bob was looking at a magazine someone had left out on a table in the dayroom. It had photos of Vietnam. He was looking in particular at this photo of a GI walking through a swamp who was clutching someone else's decapitated head by its black hair. The soldier's face was wide and mean, and the face on the head, though dead, almost looked like it was smiling—that smile had been what caught Bob's eye. Bob wondered where the GI might be bringing the head, or what the purpose would be in doing so, not to mention what the dead man was smiling about. Just then, a new guy was ushered into the ward by an orderly in white.

He was just about the biggest toughest black guy Bob had ever seen and yet when he crossed the room, Bob didn't feel afraid of him. This guy certainly didn't give off that same vibe everybody else in here did—people in here either made Bob nervous or they weren't like people at all, they were more like placeholders where people had once been. No, instead he stepped into the ward so calm you'd have thought he was in charge of the joint. He was a patient, though; he wore pajamas.

Then Bob realized: he was the GI from the photograph.

If *that* wasn't a sign from the universe, he didn't know what was. Bob later introduced himself. The GI's name was Bart, and he became Bob's first real friend at Herrick Hospital.

During their months hanging out together—eating meals and taking pills, playing cards and sitting in the shade by the blacktop—Bart and Bob talked about anything and everything. Bob had started smoking cigarettes because just about everybody else did. He thought smoking was great. Sometimes during group, the smoke would be so thick that you could barely see the eyeballs of the guy sitting across from you. He thought that was hilarious.

There was an out-of-tune upright piano with some missing hammers and chipped ivories in the dayroom. Bob played it whenever they let him. Eventually they said he could play for an hour every night at nine. Whoever was around would applaud when he was done and in time some people would be there waiting for him to play before he even took a seat. He liked how the keys felt beneath his fingers and the sense that he was good at something, capable, that his dreams had not already expired.

One nurse, a black woman, always seemed to show up to hear him play. Sometimes she'd even close her eyes while she listened. He learned her name was Fay.

They began to talk each evening, and other times of day, too. She showed him the photo of her two boys she kept in her uniform pocket. She was getting divorced AND WANTED TO MARRY ME:

The orderlies were all terrified of Bart, so Fay arranged it so Bob and Bart were in a special therapy group with just her, which was great. One time all they did was watch some movie that was like *Romeo and Juliet* but in a jungle, and there was a scene where a guy made another guy's heart explode by giving him too much water. Another two nurses had joined and Bart put his arms around them. Bob put his arm around Fay and felt his fingers on her warm skin. They didn't do anything else, though, not even kiss.

He was interacting with the other patients more this time and they were teaching him A LOT ABOUT REALITY. One guy explained he ran the biggest car theft organization in San Francisco; another said he was a hired killer; another explained that he had created a machine you could fuck. Other women wanted to have sex with him but Bob didn't want to have sex with anyone yet.

Sometimes Bob would walk from his bed and into the hall and two or three weeks would pass, just like that, and he had a suntan. Where the fuck had he been.

Once, a woman in a neck brace walked up, took Bob's picture, and walked away. She could have been Lydia Treeantopolis's older sister. She left flanked by dudes who, by their look, were CIA.

One time when he was in seclusion, the Asian guy in the next cell over broke through glass three inches thick. A HERO IN MY BOOK:

:::::

"Get up," said a voice.

Little slivers of daylight fell through the blanket pulled over his face. First thing Bob remembered was that Bart was gone. He'd gotten out yesterday.

"Get up!" the voice said again.

Bart had made a promise to Bob before he left. He said he would tell people about what was happening inside Herrick Hospital. He'd get help. Go to the press or something.

"I said get up!"

The blanket was ripped away and Bob looked at the bright room. It was the same as it had been yesterday and the day before and the day before that. Same fluorescents humming, same yellowing walls, same cages on the windows in case you got the urge to fly away.

"I said get up!"

"What the fuck, man," Bob said.

"I said get up. Don't want to miss the bus."

"Bus?"

"That's what I said."

Bob got up. He walked down the hall and followed the others who were walking downstairs.

The line of patients waiting to get on the bus went halfway down the block and into the hospital's lobby. He got in line and tapped the back ahead of him.

"Hey, man, you know where we're headed?" Bob asked.

"Nah," the guy said.

Orderlies in white circled and nipped like herding dogs at the slow-moving line. After a while Bob made it through the glass doors. He looked down to the bus. The fog had burned off already. He worried about his skin in the sun. Bart would have known. This was terrible luck, that Bart was gone on this, of all days.

Bob turned to the guy behind him. "You know where we're going?" he asked.

The guy didn't look like he heard.

Bob pulled a cigarette from the pack in his pocket. "Got a light?" He tapped the guy ahead of him again.

"Here." He lit Bob's with his.

"Thanks, man." Bob exhaled and felt that fleeting pleasure of the morning's first smoke.

"My buddy Bart would have known where we're headed," Bob said, and the guy nodded. Bob continued: "Knew all sorts of shit, Bart. He got out yesterday. You ever heard of a field trip before? I mean, you been on one, man?" A lot of the guys in Herrick had been in there longer than Bob, some longer than he'd been alive.

"Not that I been on," the guy replied.

"Alright, cool."

By the time he got on the bus, the only spot left was up front near the orderlies, who were all mucking around with one another.

The bus lurched away from the curb and moved slowly up the block. Bob studied the power lines and shining storefronts. People were entering and exiting buildings and cars, completely unaware of the bus and its passengers and the reality in which they were living.

They began climbing up the little dark streets of the Berkeley Hills, passing curbs and corners where Bob had hung out as a kid.

Bob wondered whether Bart would make good on

his promise, actually get help. He fantasized about how it would go after Bart went to the papers and told them the reality of what was going on inside Herrick Hospital. He pictured crowds of protestors gathering outside of Herrick Hospital, pumping their fists, thrusting their signs. He pictured the caged windows shattering, glass cascading onto the asphalt, cigarette smoke wafting out into the blue. He pictured the doors flung open and men in pajamas wandering blinking into the lot.

People in pajamas finding their wives and parents and kids.

Fresh air.

Everyone falling.

Everyone realizing that nothing separated us ever.

The bus was parking. Bob recognized where they'd ended up: Tilden Park. He'd gone to Tilden as a kid, to the little amusement park and petting zoo there. The amusement park had an old rickety steam train for children to ride. He remembered the stench and sound of its belching, and how when it turned corners he could slide down the slick green-painted seats and crush his sisters, who would shriek at him to stop.

One time, his mom had brought the kids' pet rabbits to the petting zoo and let them go when no one was looking. She must have been tired of the kids having rabbits. He wasn't sure whether they'd still be here.

How long did a rabbit live?

He got off the bus. The other patients were wandering off. He wasn't sure what he was supposed to do. He set off along a shaded path, so drugged he may as well have been asleep.

He passed a fenced enclosure where toddlers stumbled up to beasts with palms of feed and mothers and nannies cooed patiently by. He found a bench in the shade that faced one of the steam train's curves. Soon the train came roaring, its little cars full of shrieking passengers. He watched their big delighted mouths and eyes.

Did they have time to notice a long-haired dude chain-smoking in his pajamas?

It was quiet for a while and then another train came.

Bob remembered back to a time he'd come to Tilden Park and done acid. He remembered he and the other kids he was with had watched a rainstorm come in—a wall of water like someone was pulling a curtain across the world. "Run!" Bob had yelled and they all did and somehow avoided getting wet and then watched, mouths gaping, as a rainbow stretched across the heavens.

He sat some hours watching the trains pass every few minutes. Then the orderlies came around and snapped at him to get back in line. He and the other patients slowly got back on the bus.

"What was the point of that?" Bob wondered aloud. "What was the goddamn point of *that*?"

That evening Bob was sitting on the sofa in the dayroom. On the news, a big black guy surrounded by protestors was talking into a reporter's microphone. It took Bob a moment to recognize Bart, in part because he was wearing fatigues, not pajamas.

What was Bart doing on TV?

He was flanked by about twenty-five people. They were holding signs; one said SHRINMKS KILL::: Bart was yelling something.

Bart had kept his promise!

Maybe, Bob realized, it wasn't a coincidence that that morning, of all mornings, they had put together a field trip!

Nothing else came of that, as far as Bob knew.

He never saw Bart again.

His dad was back from Singapore and visited Bob at Herrick. He gave him a deck of cards that had some language on them Bob couldn't read; someone stole them later anyway. His dad sat with Bob and the rest of them while a movie called *Mutiny on the Bounty* played.

Bob didn't really know what to say to the guy.

At some point later that summer, his mom got permission to take Bob to Lake L'Homme Dieu. When Dr. G. first told him about the plan, Bob had assumed he was being fucked with. But no, his mom said on the phone, it was real.

When the day finally arrived, his fingers barely remembered how to tie laces.

An orderly walked him down the hall and to the elevator.

The doors parted and there was his mom in the lobby, smiling.

"Hi, Bobby."

"Hi, Mom."

Did he look different to her?

He followed her out the glass door and onto

the street, shielding his eyes with his hands. His sister Debbie was becoming a teenager; her hair was flaxen and long. She gave him a brief hug. And his sister Heather looked practically grown, chestnut hair to her shoulders.

They were driving two cars to Minnesota. He'd drive with his mom, and Heather was following in her little Karmann Ghia.

His mom had two new dogs, a Gordon Setter and a corgi mix, and their salty breath was all over him as he climbed into her backseat.

They had his meds so high he could barely think. He had no idea how he'd manage for the thousands of miles of driving, not to mention how he'd interact with people once they got to the lake.

He sighed.

They drove out of Berkeley and onto the freeway. He tried to ask the names of the dogs but had trouble with his thoughts, words.

His mom turned down the radio. "Bob?" she asked.

He changed his mind about saying anything at all, and leaned his head against the glass.

After a few minutes his mom turned up the radio again.

They camped in the desert that night. The next morning, they hadn't been on the road long when his mom, looking at the rearview mirror, remarked that something was going on with Heather.

Bob turned around and saw her emergencies flashing and heard honking. They both pulled over and his mom walked back toward Heather's smoking hood.

Bob and Debbie got out of the car and joined them. Tears were pouring from beneath Heather's sunglasses. She and his mom yelled at one another for a while and Heather stormed away down the highway to find a phone, to call her dad, to beg for money to fix her engine. His mom acted mad, but they all knew that was the only solution.

It took all day to fix it, and then another three to cross the Minnesota border.

Finally: there were the streets of downtown Alexandria. There was Big Ole the Viking and the goofy golf course and the place with the trampolines. As they bumbled down the dirt lane, he could see a glimmer of water through the birch green.

And then there was the whole of Lake L'Homme Dieu, and the white cottage, and his grandma and grandpa and cousins coming up from the dock.

If he were able to feel anything, Bob would have cried.

Tommy must have been six inches taller.

Bob wondered what he looked like to his relatives.

Had they heard about what had happened to him?

During dinner, Grandpa Ray's hands quivered, Bob noticed, as he lifted a fork to his lips.

Heather and Jane were laughing about something and the dogs were patrolling for scraps and Bob was caught up in the unreality of all this. The whole room—the warping old windows, the scratchy sisal floors, the orange light—felt like a movie set, like they were playing a scene in which an extended family ate dinner in a summer cottage by a lake. Bob had been living in a different movie for so long. He realized Herrick felt more like home, the staff and patients felt more like his family.

Bob looked to his grandfather; guy hardly spoke. He realized the two of them had more in common than he did with anyone else at the table.

Bob couldn't fish or swim or water-ski like he would in summers past. He reminded himself often he had to be careful in the sun because of the meds.

He tried to catch up with his relatives but it was tough. He was always distracted trying to figure out what other people were thinking—what was going on inside their heads. It was something he used to be able to know without asking but now it was harder, somehow.

Interacting with everyone was also difficult because no one wanted to hear about what had happened to him over the last year. No one was interested in Herrick Hospital, or his coma, or what happened to him at Sunny Hills—the energy ray that had come down from the heavens.

They ignored him, politely as they could.

Not that he felt upset about this. He couldn't feel sad same as he couldn't feel happy. Bob's lungs filled with air and his heart beat and his legs walked but he wasn't a person. He was A LIVING ZOMBIE: JUST A BREATHING SURVIVING ENTITY WITH NO AMOTIONS.

At night, listening to his family breathe through the cottage's thin walls, he thought about how few things he had owned. He thought about how few friends he had kept. He thought about how he'd gotten to see Hendrix live, and how Hendrix was dead now. Outside, the loons wailed. The facts of his life floated by in his mind, sad facts like trash and leaves floating down a creek to the sea, and the sea is as true and incomprehensible a fact as a given life, or a given brain.

One day they gassed up the speedboat, packed picnic baskets, and sputtered out onto the water. Even on a hot day like this it was always cooler on the lake. Red and blue dragonflies zipped up to them and away. Throughout the day, Bob noticed how old his grandpa looked.

When they were back ashore, walking up to the little white cottage, Bob turned to his mom and said, "I've been thinking. Grandpa should get more exercise."

"My dad?" she asked.

They scraped their feet on the green plastic doormat. As his mom opened the screen door, they heard the scream.

Grandpa Ray was facedown on the bed, not on the bed all the way, but only half on the bed, and his head was cocked to the side funny and he was still.

They shouted his name, "Grandpa!" and "Dad!"

"Don't touch him!" his mom screamed as Bob approached the body and everybody was red and crying.

The funeral was in Minneapolis and their departure from the lake was sudden. He was overwhelmed by the feeling that the universe had warned him that Grandpa Ray was about to die.

At the service, Bob leaned against the wallpaper and tried to feel like everybody else. After, he and his cousins went to see The Who at a coliseum but it was too loud and Bob's head was throbbing. He didn't know yet but that was the last time he'd ever go to Lake L'Homme Dieu.

He didn't remember how he got back to Herrick Hospital.

Maybe he flew.

Before long, he again fell into the place's routine. He was impressed as ever by the guys in there who were veterans. Listening to their stories, he understood the CRAZYNESS OF NAM. One guy would recite, bawling, the things he'd done. HE WAS EXTREEMLY SUICIDLE but, unable to kill himself, just wanted to be left alone.

Sometimes being left alone was all that any of them had.

During one of their pointless meetings, Dr. G. told Bob he thought Bob had ten thousand personalities. Bob didn't give a fuck about the guy or anything he had to say. All he cared about was living through each day, counting down the days until he turned eighteen. That's when they couldn't hold him anymore. That's when he'd be able to walk out of this place.

A Real Shocker

Bob's friends who'd known him the two summers before he went to Herrick Hospital, the guys who went on those backpacking trips down in the Sierras, all called him by a nickname, "Loooooogie." They all said it high and long and loud, "Loooooooogie."

I finally asked one of them what it meant.

It was something Bob used to say, he said, a noise he used to make. He'd say it to the birds. He'd screech like them, too.

They were so joyous as they remembered Loogie. A lot of them were from Ohio, but Loogie was cool, he was from Berkeley. He was small, but he could carry a pack as well as anyone else. A great climber. One guy raved about how, using just a stone cooker, Loogie baked the very best pies. ("You come back from climbing all day and had a Loogie apple pie, you were sitting pretty good," he said.) They of course remembered the big fight with the local guys—which they recalled had been after a dance—and how it was this guy Tom who got hit with the first rock. They remembered going to some house and watching the moon landing.

He was different that second year they were there, they said. Some knew or figured he was smoking weed.

His friends from Berkeley mostly wanted to talk about how he played guitar. How he played just like Hendrix. How you'd be going by this mom's house and the whole street would be quaking, how he'd absolutely *nail* the riffs.

His old friend Dave remembered when they played that weird show in Oakland—the van that drove them there, how the place was full of guys who were maybe Hell's Angels. "Really totally an alien place," he said.

His friend whose name was also Bob described how talented Bob was. Often he didn't have a band to play with, so he'd play all of a song's parts himself. "He'd be doing all the bass and the drum parts as well as the guitar parts. It was quite a style." It was a style, he added, that made it hard for Bob to play with others.

He didn't seem to remember being as close with Bob as Bob had described. None of the guys I spoke with copped to remembering this or that particular trip or time getting high.

None of them really knew what became of him. It was hard to keep track of a lot of things back then. Some knew vaguely that something had happened. They guessed it had something to do with the drugs.

"The thing about psychedelics is you have to give in to the void sometimes, and hopefully, the void will spit you back out," the other Bob said. "I have a feeling he had a hard time getting back out." He told a story—something he'd heard, he hadn't been there personally—about how my uncle had had an especially rough acid trip once when he was in his dad's bedroom. There were these mirrors in there that faced each other: "You looked one way and you could see off into infinity. I think Bob got stuck in there."

No one else I found remembered anything like that. I asked Gene whether his bedroom had two mirrors that faced each other. He said no, though his bedroom up at the condo at Tahoe did have doors with mirrors on them. My uncle's friend Dave pointed out something I'd noticed, too, which was that "Room Full of Mirrors" is a famous Hendrix song.

Bob's only friend I found who remembered actually seeing him in a hospital was Tony, from the old neighborhood. Tony admired Bob, who was a year older. He excitedly remembered their boyhood adventures, including the time they went into the City to a strip club and somehow got served. By Tony's recollection, they were even younger than Bob remembered; they'd been twelve or thirteen. He laughed, saying he'd told that story so many times because it was so unbelievable. He said Bob was probably his "best friend" back then, but then his family moved districts around junior high and he saw Bob less after that.

One day when he was about sixteen, though, Tony's mother told him Bob had been hospitalized and was asking to see him. Said Bob was having "flashbacks." Tony got in his brand-new VW Beetle and drove down to Herrick Hospital (he had no recollection of going to visit Bob in Marin).

They sat across from each other at a big table. Bob was in pajamas. His hair was long, and his words were jumbled.

"My head was spinning, trying to take it all in," Tony said. "Here I am just a kid still, so it was a real shocker. The last time I'd seen Bob it was the old Bob, and all of a sudden there's this new Bob." He added that he didn't know whether the difference was whatever Bob had taken or whatever they had him on.

For a moment, Tony confused me with my mom, whom he'd also known growing up. I reminded him that I was Sandy, not Debbie.

Of course, he said. Then he paused. "So you never knew him?" he realized aloud. "Before?"

Bob's relatives' understanding of what happened to him was only slightly better. His cousins on his mom's side remembered the summer he came to L'Homme Dieu and was changed. Some of them knew—or later knew—that he was taking medications. They likewise were quick to say they didn't know whether the difference was him or what he was taking. "He was so uncomfortable to be around because he was so heavily medicated," one cousin told me.

Another recalled Bob saying that he'd been abducted by

aliens. The cousin didn't know what to make of that, thought maybe he'd been reading too many comic books.

But they didn't remember whatever was happening with Bob being a topic of conversation; nobody recalled hearing the word "schizophrenia."

Almost nobody in the family seems to have known this was his diagnosis.

When I talked to people about my uncle, they often asked me quietly yet eagerly—as if they'd always wanted to ask—what he *had*.

Many then offered their theories as to what had caused it. Other than the drugs, the most popular contender was the divorce. Some blamed the hospital itself.

Relatives would often volunteer who else in the family was crazy, but there was nothing I was able to confirm. All were accusations flung over the chasm of the divorce, as if to say that those other people were who the bad part came from.

FAMOUSE

He awoke the morning he turned eighteen. Ate off a final tray. Waited. His mom and cousin Jane from Minnesota showed up on the ward. He learned she'd gotten pregnant on a backpacking trip with Heather in Morocco.

In the lobby, Fay dabbed at the corner of her eye with a tissue. He hugged her goodbye. He knew she got it, though, she understood why Bob was leaving.

An orderly stuck out his hand to shake Bob's goodbye THINKING ALL WAS FORGIVEN, but Bob just looked at the guy. He followed his family out the front doors.

He stepped onto the asphalt into a green California winter's day, that same parking lot that he had crossed, confused, at sixteen.

It was 1972. Bob was a man, and finally free.

The compounds quickly drained from his blood and his brain. He began to recover the sense of himself that he had lost since he was first brought to Herrick. He became aware of the quickness of his thoughts and the limberness of his tongue. The weight he'd gained hung off him like borrowed clothing. He recognized the texture of his own skin again, and his smell, and he no longer had to cower in the sun. The marvel that was the sun!

Without the drugs slowing him down, he realized that it was his job to turn his life around, that nobody was going to do it for him, and that he was capable of doing it. And the world, it seemed, was interested in making up for all the shit it'd dealt him these last few years.

His mom helped him buy his first car, a 1963 Grand Prix. He drove over and got himself enrolled at an adult school so he'd get a high school diploma, and took classes at Merritt Community College in ceramics, oceanography, and electronics. For the first time in awhile, he was learning. He loved ceramics especially, getting his nail beds dirty, making girls in class laugh, coming home with pots. He loved, too, messing with electronics. Or getting to go out on a boat into the marsh with his oceanography class. They would stick a tool down in the mud to measure the sediment in the bay.

He'd moved into the apartment his mom had built out downstairs and she wanted him to start paying rent, so he needed to get a job. Fortunately, he met a neighbor, a guy named Don, who was a logger. Don showed Bob how to hold a chainsaw and settle its racing teeth into the flesh of a tree.

Bob convinced his mom to help him buy a chainsaw of his own and spent a weekend helping this crew of guys clear-cut a lot of eucalyptus that had died in a recent frost. All over the Bay Area that winter there were flash-frozen eucalyptus that needed felling. Bob told the crew's boss that he'd work for three days for free and if the guy didn't like him he'd split. The foreman agreed and after the three days, Bob was hired. He got along with the rest of the felling crew and eventually made $8.50 an hour.

The goal was to work with them only until he could finally start making a living as a guitarist. Sunny Hills had sent over not one but two guitars in apology for the one that'd been stolen by a kid named Johnny Crooks—no joke.

He'd started this band with these two black veterans named Tom and Warren. They picked up a drummer, Henry, two conga players, this dude Dorian they met in a park, and this Mexican guy Francisco, and finally, a keyboardist named Wayne. Looking at them, you had whites, blacks, and a Mexican; they called themselves Choice of Colors.

Bob liked being back in his childhood home. He liked being around his mom and his sisters again, not to mention their friends, and Jane, and then her new baby girl. These people didn't judge him for what had happened to him or the things he'd seen.

He didn't go see his dad; he didn't want to. He had heard his dad had some new girlfriend he was marrying, a former student who had two daughters already.

Bob would sit out on the porch, strum his

guitar. The front door opened and slammed and footsteps pattered up and down the stairs and the sun sparkled off into his blue eyes.

This era when everything was working out almost made the last few years feel worth it. Or, rather, had he not been through all that he had, he certainly wouldn't have loved those days as much as he now could.

One day, a guy who communicated with Bob only through the mail hired him to clear a lot of eucalyptus by himself. Don had helped set it up. Every day Bob was to fell forty trees, strip their branches, and slice up each trunk.

When Bob showed up to begin the job, there was already a crew working the lot, a group of prisoners, by the looks of them. Bob knew they had no right to be there, but they ended up saving him tons of work. He finished the job early and received $1,500 from the guy through the mail. He'd asked only that the lot be cleared, so Bob got to sell the firewood himself and made even more.

Which was great for Choice of Colors. He bought a piece of equipment called an Echoplex. Tom meanwhile had learned to play electric bass and they'd bought him an amp. At the end of the year, Bob took a test and got a high school diploma, but he had to drop out of community college because he spent too much time working and practicing. They were booking weddings and parties and playing a club down in Oakland on Saturday nights. Bob loved the band, loved the guys, loved how Tom especially was always looking out for him.

They were setting up to play a show in Oakland once when someone dimmed the lights. People stepped back, and in the circle of space stood a woman, a woman who lit the ends of two sticks and began to dance between the swirls of fire. Each pass of the fire roared as she swayed her hips.

Bob tried to keep focused on his sound, but he couldn't help but study the woman's hips and her hair and her hands and the way gasoline drips were gathering in a pattern on either side of her bare feet, a pattern visible only as the two fires blazed past the floor.

After, standing out behind the club, the sweat on his back cooled in the night air. He dragged on a cigarette and wondered how big Choice of Colors might get. He pictured those two fires whipping by, and the woman and her dance, and all the faces looking to him and the other guys and their music. Bob knew in that moment that little separated him from a god.

Back inside, the fire dancer came up to him, thanked him for playing. He'd never been close to something that beautiful.

Bob still hadn't had sex. He avoided talking about sex with the guys in the band or the felling crew and hoped they assumed he'd had it; they were obsessed with it, it seemed, always talking about banging one chick after another. Bob still wanted to be in love before he did something like that. It made him uncomfortable, the idea of people having sex with lots of others.

Despite this, he had strolled into a porno theater down in Berkeley one day. The place creeped him out, smelled wrong, and yet he went back once in awhile.

Girls made passes at him occasionally. Once he was home, and his sister Debbie walked in with this girl Daisy. Daisy was the first girl he'd kissed. Daisy had been over at his house when he was about fourteen and they had started to kiss. As they did, Bob had remembered Lydia Treeantopolis. He realized he didn't love Daisy like he'd loved Lydia. He stopped kissing her, and he told her she had to go. He looked at her through the window by the door as she sat crying, waiting for her mom to pick her up.

Standing now with Daisy in his mom's kitchen, he realized she'd heard of Choice of Colors.

She asked whether he could get her into a show.

"Nah, man, you're too young," Bob said, "Hell, I'm too young to be in there." Which was true; he was just eighteen turning nineteen, but nobody seemed to care. Between sets he usually sat at the bar and sucked down Schlitz after Schlitz.

That weekend, the bouncer said some Berkeley High chicks came by trying to get in, saying they knew him. Bob lied that he had no idea who they were.

He was relieved they'd been turned away.

Inside the club, he took a long pull of his beer and pictured Daisy crying by the door.

One night a guy from the logging company was at the bar and he kept waving to Bob and Bob kept waving back. Bob didn't realize the guy was putting beers on Bob's tab, so Bob was stuck with the whole bill. Not that he cared. Things were looking up. He and some of the other guys started talking about getting the money together to record an album.

Choice of Colors played a gig in a park soon after but nobody showed. Then Tom got in a fight with some random guy. They decided to play anyway and Bob saw cars slowing to hear them, and after that people were starting to talk about them around town. Two black women joined the group, singers. They played a house party where Bob was the only white person there, and they continued pulling a good crowd at the club. One time their show was so good, people spontaneously cried.

Everything started to fall apart when some terrorists killed his mom's boss. Bob had come home and found her in the kitchen, crying.

Then Bob's boss told him the felling crew was moving up to Oregon. He invited Bob along. Bob said he was thinking of learning about computers instead and the guy had no idea what he was talking about.

Then Bob caught the Jewish dude who lived in the apartment downstairs rifling through some of his stuff. He asked Bob if he could have some of his baseball cards, which were in a box. Bob said sure. Years later, he would realize how valuable the cards were—hundreds of thousands of dollars—and figured LEAVE IT TO A JEW TO RIP YOU OFF.

His mom had to kick those tenants out later anyway, because they came home drunk all the time.

Without a job, Bob spent his days watching the news or just walking around. Perhaps because he was older, or perhaps because he was friends with some vets now, he took more interest in what was going on in the streets.

One day he was passing by the Berkeley amphitheater as some political concert was about to start. A lot of people were naked. That week he had written down what he was calling A WPORLD CONSTITUTION. It was on a slip of paper in his pocket. He'd written "FOR STREEKING PURPOSES ONLY" on the outside and inside it said:

THE BLACK CULTURE:HAS THE BEAUTY TO MAKE THE ORDER AND KEEP THE PEACE.
THE CHINESE AND JAPANESE RACES:HAVE THE TALENT TO MIX THE FRUIT AND CREATE THE PLANNING OF THE UNIVERSE
THE WHITE MAN: HAS NOTHING BUT THE PERSONALITY TO HARMONIZE THE THOUGHTS OF THE PLANET.
THE INDIAN: IS THE WISEST OF RELIGION

He sprinted onstage, handed the constitution to a guy with a mic, and ran off. He'd gone down the trail a ways when he heard the CROWD GIVE A HUGE ROAR OF ACCEPTANCE and some naked hippie dude was running toward him.

"Where are you going?" the hippie asked.

"Dunno, man," Bob said.

"You can't leave," he said, YOUR FAMOUSE:

Nobody had ever called him anything like that before.

Which was why he decided to get active in politics.

At his mom's place he found a stack of paper and some envelopes. He sat himself down at the kitchen table, flattened out one sheet, and wrote the first of what would become many letters.

He wrote letters to local newspapers and television and radio stations. He wrote letters to scientists and celebrities and world leaders. He wrote to the subcommittee investigating Watergate and officials in Moscow. He covered the envelopes in stamps. He put his return address as the TERRERIST PARTY or THE NAM EXPERT or THE MUNICH TERRERIST and walked around Berkeley distributing the letters in different mailboxes so they were harder to trace back to him.

He saw his dad one day when he was out mailing letters, recognized him behind the wheel. He couldn't be sure whether his dad recognized him, too, but Bob thought he did, and thought he recognized the look on his face as one of disgust.

The light changed and the car pulled away.

His mom's next-door neighbor was a lady named Mrs. D., who was also Jewish. One time the band was over in the garage practicing and Mrs. D. came knocking, yelling that it was too loud. Bob told the band to keep playing, but right then his mom pulled up. She got out of her car waving her hands, exclaiming, "Bob, you need to cut this out right now!"

She took Mrs. D.'s arm and began apologizing to her.

Bob couldn't believe his mom would take this woman's side instead of his, especially because the band was the only thing he had going for him now.

He understood his mom less and less these days. A few years ago she had dated this used-car salesman, Mac; he'd lived awhile in the apartment downstairs and even let Bob borrow his motorcycle once. As far as Bob could tell, Mac treated her well and even took her out to dinner sometimes.

Now, though, she was seeing this black veteran who'd written some book. He was always trying to talk to Bob, even if Bob was trying to pass quickly by.

"How are you, Bob?" the book author would ask. He'd ask about Bob's plans and what was on his mind. Somehow he always steered the conversation back to his opinion that Bob should go to St. Mary's College, where his son went. He told Bob he should become a chaplain in the air force like him.

Bob shifted his weight and waited until he could finally leave.

His mom wouldn't even stand up for her son and explain that he was in a successful band.

Ever since his mom had sided with Mrs. D., Choice of Colors had to practice at Tom's place. Bob got there early one day.

He sat down at Tom's kitchen table and lit

a cigarette. Tom was in the next room. Bob started telling Tom about his fear that his mom was going to marry that book author. As he spoke, Bob realized he didn't have time to just sit around like this.

"You know what, man, I'm going to get going," Bob said, smashing out his cigarette.

"Stick around here for a minute, Bob," Tom said.

What did Tom want with him?

"Nah, man, I gotta get out of here."

"Just a minute—" Tom looked like he was going to get in between Bob and the door, so Bob sprinted across the kitchen and down the drive and sidewalk.

He jumped in his car and jammed the key in the ignition and sped up the street.

There was the long cry of glass and metal and his head was slamming against the steering wheel and there was smoke and he hurt, he hurt, he hurt.

Red lights and blue lights.

Red lights and blue.

Another car was wrapped around his.

Minutes or hours later, through the fog of everything, he saw his mom there talking to the cops.

And then he saw his dad.

For a while Bob was laid up on his mom's couch, trying to breathe despite the pain and the stitches, trying to figure out why his bandmates were avoiding him, trying to figure out how he was going to get anywhere now that his car was totaled.

Patty Hearst was all over the news. She was a rich white kid from Berkeley who'd been kidnapped by the SLA and now she had joined her kidnappers.

Sometimes he would pick up a sheet of paper and write a letter to the anchor telling him or her what to say. Later, when the anchor spoke the line he had sent them, he would laugh.

Anyway, this was what he did until his mom finally kicked him out for owing her rent. Bob called up his dad and asked to stay with him.

His dad's new house was over on the other side of the Caldecott Tunnel. Place was huge. Bob was always sure to take off his shoes lest he get something on the carpets. He didn't want to piss off his new stepmom, Agnes.

They let him sleep in a bedroom downstairs. His new stepsisters were younger; their dad lived back east still. They seemed fine. Maybe it was because they were little but he felt all the time like he was a kid again.

Sometimes his dad let him borrow a car. He drove one day down to the library and was wandering through the stacks when, for no reason at all (or maybe for a very good reason), he reached out and opened up a legal book. Right there was written a law about how when a kidnapped person goes along with the kidnapper, the kidnapper can no longer be charged with a crime. In other words, now that Patty Hearst had joined the SLA, the police were investigating a crime that wasn't.

That he'd happened upon this law was incredible.

Bob copied it down and hurried back to his dad's house. He wrote a letter explaining his findings to the mayor of Oakland, signing it "The Terrorist Party."

On the radio they were talking about Patty, because always everybody was talking about her.

Back at home, he picked up the phone to call in.

"Have you heard the SLA theme song yet?" he asked the woman who answered.

"There's an SLA theme song?" she asked.

And like that he was on the air.

"Yeah, man, I just wanted to know if you've heard the SLA theme song yet," he repeated to the host.

A few days later, the SLA released a new theme song.

Soon after, again on the radio, they announced that a member of the terrorist party had just proved that Patty Hearst's kidnapping was legal.

Bob laughed loud.

THIS WAS FUN:

Bob went into his dad and Agnes's master bathroom. He looked in the mirror and braided his hair. He took a tube of Agnes's lipstick and smudged a crimson splotch between his eyes. He took a knife from the kitchen. He walked down through the neighborhood.

Before long he saw a couple of women jogging.

"Me no want food!" he screamed at them, laughing and waving the knife above his head. It was funny because the Hearsts had tried to negotiate with the SLA—who'd demanded they donate millions in food to the poor—and when they had, people had rioted and thrown cabbages and bananas and stuff. Bob took off his shirt and yelled again: "Me no want food! Meeee no want fooooood!"

He was expecting them to laugh, but what they did instead was scream.

He turned around and headed back up to the house. He was in his basement room when Agnes came down, walked in without even knocking, said he needed to go see Dr. G. right away.

He got on his ten-speed and decided it'd be fastest to just take the freeway.

He zipped through town and onto the on-ramp and was soon pedaling alongside cars going sixty, and then through the Caldecott Tunnel.

He was going as fast as the cars somehow, and they didn't even honk at him. He got into Berkeley, thinking he must have made history or something, bicycling like that.

His dad drove up, PISSED AS HELL. He loaded Bob and his bike in the car. Bob was sure he was going back to Herrick Hospital, but instead they went to a different hospital over in Walnut Creek.

Things were different at LA CASA VIA; he could tell right away. The hallways were clean and bright. On the closed unit—he was only there for a week—the staff told him over and over again that things were going to be fine. They addressed him by his full name. This one nurse was hanging out and he told her all about all the CRAZY stuff he'd been up to.

She just laughed and shook her head.

She told him again he was going to be alright.

On the open ward, there were arts and crafts and a patio and two pianos. He was free to wander the corridors as he pleased, free to say what was on his mind.

His new shrink, Dr. Widroe, actually seemed to listen when Bob expressed his hatred of the medications. He even ate the same food that the patients did in the cafeteria, though Bob learned it was considered rude for him to sit at the doctors' table.

During therapy was when you'd find out who someone was or what they were up to. You could never truly predict who had lived what kind of life. Some patients had done shit that had landed them front-page headlines in the newspapers. Others were immensely rich. Others had been homeless, or had come from other countries. Like this one girl—just about the quietest, sweetest girl he'd ever met—admitted one day that she murdered her parents and burned their bodies in the fireplace. Or this thirteen-year-old black girl who until a few months ago had lived her entire life in a closet. There were also celebrities WHO WANTED TO REST, PEOPLE LIKE THAT:

At the end of each therapy session at La Casa Via, Bob felt connected to everyone else in a way that he hadn't before experienced. There was no swearing or fighting or threatening or teasing, like there'd sometimes been at Herrick or at Sunny Hills. In general, it was understood at La Casa Via that if you acted out or stole or anything, you'd be thrown back onto the closed unit—with seclusion and restraints—so Bob tried to keep the peace.

Widroe put him on Prolixin and lithium and Artane and soon he was feeling PRETTY CONFERTIBLE AND LOOSE. There were outings all the time—to public swimming pools, baseball games, movies, restaurants, picnics. He could get permission to leave, too, walk down the block to buy cigarettes.

He was playing guitar in the dayroom one day and this chick walked in and sat nearby. When he finished one song, she smiled and looked at her feet.

"Do you play?" Bob asked her. She shook her head and smiled even more.

"I'm Bob," he said, standing up and leaning down to shake her hand.

"Wendy," she said.

She was Japanese, and twenty-three, and in there, Bob learned, to kick heroin. She was super high energy and sunny and CRAZY about him. Before long, he had what he felt was his first real girlfriend.

The staff at La Casa Via didn't mind if Bob and Wendy walked with their arms around one another, and they weren't quick to bust them for being alone in Bob's room making out—just making out; they never had sex. One nurse even said one day as they passed, "What a good-looking couple!"

Or another time he was in this math class and the teacher was explaining some addition trick where she had five rows of six numbers each, and said that you could multiply them by adding the rows together. For some reason, the answer was already in Bob's head, so he blurted it out.

"Did you figure that out just now?" she asked.

"Yeah." Bob was likewise astonished.

The teacher gave another set and the same thing: after about two seconds Bob was speaking the answer aloud. The other students tittered.

"Let's see if you can beat me," the teacher said now, rising, copying another onto the board, and as she was writing the last number Bob said the answer. Wendy was standing in the doorway waiting for Bob. The teacher turned and said, YOUR BOYFRIEND IS A GENIOSE:

She had been so kind, his first girlfriend, Wendy. Didn't make him feel bad when weird stuff would happen to him, like when he'd spend the whole day thinking it was Sunday and realize it was Tuesday. Or when he'd wander the hospital's passages all day looking for someone and, once he gave up, find them standing right there.

Once he saw a thing on television about how some scientists had discovered a new kind of energy created when you blast really hot air and really cold air at one another. During his letter-writing days, Bob remembered, he had written some scientists telling them they should do exactly that. He'd told them to call it waterized electricity and that's what they were calling it on television. Bob told Wendy all about it. He couldn't tell how she took the news.

Or this other time, this dude George who was friends with his sister Heather called him up and asked if Bob could help him out with something. George was a 'Nam vet and a boxer and Bob said sure and caught a bus to Berkeley. Turned out what George wanted was for Bob to get rid of some guy who had been hanging around and bothering him, this other vet named Johnny. Right away, Johnny interested Bob a lot.

"I remember you from the war," Johnny said to Bob. Bob had no idea what the guy meant, but felt, somehow, that Johnny knew Bob better than he knew himself.

A whole day passed in what felt like one inhalation. At sunset Bob drove George's car over to the airport to drop Johnny off; he was headed to New York on a military plane and wanted Bob to go with him. Bob said he couldn't.

THAT GUY WAS A REAL TRIP:

When Bob got back to La Casa Via, the same chick he had seen at Herrick Hospital, the one with the neck brace who looked like Lydia Treeantopolis's older sister, showed up again. This time she was flanked by guys in suits and trench coats and she was holding a baby.

He told Wendy about George and Johnny, and about the woman in the neck brace.

Sometimes he'd wonder if he'd been other places without knowing, BUT WENDY KEPT ME IN REALITY:

Sometimes on his way back from buying cigarettes, he'd stop off at the maternity ward of the hospital across the boulevard.

He'd go look at the plastic bassinets of newborn babies.

Study their shut eyes, thin as dimes.

Watch them squirm and breathe.

Then he'd head back to La Casa Via, work on getting well.

The Right Treatment

Had I read Bob's manuscript only up to the description of his first stay at Herrick Hospital, I might have supposed it was a screed against psychiatry as a whole. Or that he disputed the idea that there was something going on inside his brain, something that made it hard for him sometimes. But his manuscript didn't dispute this; perhaps it's what he meant when he wrote on his manuscript's cover page that he was unable to iden-tify with reality. He didn't embrace the word "schizo-phrenia," of course. The word he tended to use for himself, for how he was, was NUTS. Accordingly, he called psychiatric hos-pitals THE NUT HOUSE.

His manuscript included many positive opinions about the various facilities where he stayed—and the people who cared for him. He particularly liked the second one, which he called LA CASA VIA (it's since closed; that was the name of its street). It's important to pay attention, I think, to the aspects of the care he received that he actually found helpful.

THE PLACE WAS LIKE A RESORT, he remarked upon his first arrival there. As he did for several hospitals when describing his initial stay, he cataloged all of its amenities: THE CAFATE-RIA WAS FUN, THE UNITS WERE VERY CLEAN: THEYED MAKE YOUR BED FOR YA EVERYDAY, AND YOU COULD WARE SANYTHING YOU WANTED: THEY HAD A GREART PATIO A PIANO ROOM IN TWO ROOMS: A POOL TABLE, A PINGPONG TABLE, AN EXERCISE ROOM, AN ARTS AND

CRAFTS ROOM, A WASHER AND DRIER AND FREE TO
WALK ANYWHERE. There, he felt CARED FOR AS MUCH AS
THE PRESIDENT OF THE UNITED STATES.

He also talked about why he liked his new doctor: HE WAS
LIKE A MAFIA GUY GETTING YOUR LIFE SAVED, HE
SEEMED TO REALLY CARE AND SHOW RESPECT, NO
LIES, NO TRICKS, AND DID WHAT HE SAID HE WOULD:

It was Bob's new stepmom, Agnes, who found that second hospital—or perhaps she and Gene found it together, she couldn't
recall.

Agnes said she and Bob had met when she and Gene began
dating. Gene had been her professor in graduate school, and
she'd then worked as his secretary. She found Bob to be a "nice
young man." She recalled learning that he had been diagnosed as
"paranoid schizophrenic" a few years before, adding that she certainly agreed with the paranoid part. She believed he'd been hospitalized even younger than sixteen; she guessed he would have
been fourteen. She also recalled hearing he had undergone electroshock therapy at Herrick Hospital. Gene wasn't sure whether
that was the case; Bob made no mention of it in his manuscript.
(The controversial therapy can cause memory loss and comas.)

When she became Bob's stepmom, Agnes read everything she
could about his diagnosis. She attended a support group for relatives of people with severe mental illnesses. After, she'd talk with
Gene about what she'd learned, and they'd read things together,
too.

Agnes, like Gene, felt that Bob did his best when he took his
medications. She and Gene lamented the idea that anyone, in
particular Bob's mother, would discourage Bob from staying on
them.

Agnes did remember that when she looked for that second
doctor, she wanted someone younger than his previous one,
whom Gene also recalled was a bit old and cold. Agnes called
Dr. Widroe "the best thing ever to happen to Bob."

Like so many of his profession, Dr. Widroe decided to go into psychiatry because he was fascinated by the mind—and because he wanted to help people. As he later recounted in a self-published memoir, when he was in medical school in the mid-fifties, he decided he wanted to get some hands-on experience in his newly chosen specialty. He made the decision to spend a summer working at a public psychiatric hospital outside of Chicago.

The first day, Widroe took himself on a tour of the hospital, walking through room after cavernous room. In one, he passed sixteen men and women in broad tubs of water. They were wrapped in gray canvas. This, an attendant told him, was "hydrotherapy."

Widroe asked if they ate, and the attendant said they were fed, yes, and once a day they were placed in leather restraints and on a toilet. He asked if they ever got out of the tubs, and the attendant said yes, they were removed at night, and restrained, and then put back in them the next morning.

Widroe walked through the "wet pack" room, where pallid near-corpses were strapped with cold packs and again covered with gray canvas.

In another room was another row of unmoving patients who'd been pumped full of insulin until they fell into comas. This was called "insulin therapy."

In another, patients were given colonic irrigations, which he was told washed away the toxins that caused schizophrenia.

This public hospital was large and very overcrowded: by his estimate, it had been built for six thousand at most but housed eight thousand. Many of its patients had been involuntarily committed, meaning a court had deemed them unfit for society and put them on a blue bus. Most who went in would never leave except to go to the city morgue.

That summer, Widroe walked by so many beds, beds in which patients lay pliant, some naked—even women, he remarked. Some had had lobotomies, meaning a surgeon had damaged or excised a portion of their brains, another therapy once argued by some to cure or reduce symptoms for various diagnoses. Other patients were confined endlessly, either in cells or with straitjackets. Few, he observed, seemed to interact with actual doctors.

He watched as they waited in long lines to get electroshock therapy. Patients had been taught to hold one another down with a sheet as, one by one, they had their temples hooked up to electrodes until a grand mal seizure was induced. As soon as one patient was finished, another quickly lay on the table and was pinned by his peers beneath the sheet.

The most horrific room Widroe entered that summer was called the "Scotch douche room." He described it as a cave of green tile with two rows of high-pressure hoses set up facing each other. Widroe watched as a thrashing man in a straitjacket was brought in and strapped between the rows of nozzles.

The water was turned on.

The man stood erect with pain, eventually crumpling forward.

An attendant explained that a few hours would calm even the most violent patients.

"In my head, I knew I was witnessing torture," Widroe wrote, "but there was nothing I could do."

The mid-fifties were, coincidentally, when the population of Americans in public mental hospitals was at its highest. It's estimated that about half a million Americans then lived in such facilities. Some historians later evidenced how these populations tended to skew black and poor.

I grew up in the nineties, so it surprised me to learn that the U.S. ever had such a large public mental health care system. American Quakers had established some of our country's first asylums. The expansion of the asylum system is credited to reformers who fought tirelessly for their public support, in particular, a reformer named Dorothea Dix. In the 1840s and '50s, Dix would travel from town to town counting the number of "lunatics" and recording their condition—how many in pens, in

146

cages, in jails. She then wrote reports, which a man would read on her behalf before state legislatures (as she wasn't permitted to do so herself). In an 1843 address to the Massachusetts legislature, she apologized for the nature of the material she had to share: "*I tell what I have seen*—painful and shocking as the details often are—that from them you may feel more deeply the imperative obligation which lies upon you to prevent the possibility of a repetition or continuance of such outrages upon humanity."

In 1840, America had 18 public asylums; by 1880, there were 139. Many of these facilities were established in remote areas. Many were working farms, which some argued gave residents an occupation, a sense of purpose, and allowed them to reconnect with nature and God. ("Lunatics" were often believed to suffer from a moral failing.) As the century wore on, some asylums grew quite large, even grand, their architecture resembling that of the great American universities. Some were working factories. Whether these facilities were actually helpful to patients—and whether patients enjoyed staying in them—seems to have depended a great deal on the amount of funding available, as well as the attitudes of those charged with administering care.

As young Dr. Widroe had witnessed firsthand, by the mid-twentieth century, America's state mental hospitals were cash-strapped, bloated, and in desperate need of reform. During his brief administration, President John F. Kennedy wanted to shift the model of treating people with mental illness from one that relied on state mental hospitals to one that championed a system of community centers. It was one of the last bills he signed before he was assassinated. While historians debate the soundness of his plan, after his death, it was abandoned. Kennedy did succeed in biasing federal spending to states against mental health care. State hospitals began to shed beds, then eventually to shutter. The passage of Medicaid, which excluded coverage in state-run institutions, also contributed to this decline.

Through the latter half of the twentieth century, some conservative politicians, in particular California governor Ronald Reagan, took up the cause of cutting mental health care funding and closing mental hospitals. Proponents called this "deinstitutionalization." Such facilities were no longer necessary, the line of reasoning went; there were drugs now, ones that some argued cured psychiatric disorders. In this view, if sick people didn't take their medications, that was their problem.

In his memoir, Dr. Widroe reflected upon how fortunate he was that by the time he was practicing, the gruesome methods he witnessed at that state hospital were on their way out. Widroe, like many psychiatrists of his generation, largely credited newly available medications for this change.

Historical accounts of twentieth-century psychiatry often credit the advent of psychiatric pharmaceuticals with finally legitimizing the field. Psychiatrists had long sought to combat the notion that their specialty was somehow lesser than those of other doctors—less empirical, less glamorous. Back in the nineteenth century, psychiatrists had been nicknamed "alienists" because they had to live off in asylums in the middle of nowhere.

The first medication marketed for its "antipsychotic" or "antischizophrenic" properties was created by a French pharmaceutical company. It had been developed after a field doctor noted that a particular antihistamine appeared to do what was previously thought impossible: reduce hallucination. It was introduced in America in 1954, coincidentally the year of Bob's birth. Here it was called Thorazine.

At first Thorazine was marketed to treat alcoholism, dementia, agitation, anxiety, pain, severe asthma, emotional stress, psoriasis, gastrointestinal disorders, nausea and vomiting in children, the "emotional upset" of menopause, the "mental anguish" of cancer, and "emotional disturbances in children," as well as schizophrenia. One advertisement showed an old man with a raised cane; another showed two girls pulling at each other's hair. (America is one of three countries where advertising pharmaceuticals directly to consumers is legal.)

Soon other drugs—collectively called "neuroleptics"—riffed on this same idea. Neuroleptics impede brain function, thereby, it's thought, decreasing hallucinations and other psychiatric symptoms. These "first-generation antipsychotics" were followed by a "second generation" or "atypical antipsychotics." Such drugs were widely understood to work differently for all patients; no one treatment worked for everybody. Whenever a new drug was released, it was invariably heralded as less deleterious and even more miraculous than its predecessors.

Thorazine was one of the pharmaceutical blockbusters of the twentieth century; other neuroleptic hits have followed. In recent decades, the pharmaceutical industry has become one of the most profitable industries overall in America. Rates of mental illness diagnosis have gone up, both for adults and for children, and mental health care, meanwhile, has become largely synonymous with medication.

In the wake of deinstitutionalization, California was the first state to see a rise in its population of homeless people diagnosed with severe mental illnesses, and its population of such people in jail and prison. The rest of the country followed suit. Much of our public mental health care system is now contained within jails and prisons (and America incarcerates people at a higher rate than all other countries on earth). At present, the largest public psychiatric facility in America is Chicago's Cook County Jail. A phrase I've read for what's happened is that we've "criminalized a disease."

The Illinois public hospital where Dr. Widroe worked was closed by that state's governor in the eighties. Today it's one of the hundreds of mostly abandoned psychiatric facilities scattered all over the country; they crumble in fields and forests on the edges of towns. They've become stomping grounds for bored teens and fodder for horror flicks and ruins photography. By the time Bob mailed me his manuscript in 2009, the ratio of psychiatric beds to patients was back at what it was in 1850.

Some celebrated the closure of these hospitals. In the late 1960s, as they closed, and amid the greater counterculturalist fervor of the era, the civil rights movement for people like Bob really began. A sociologist who's studied the movement credits the birth of "mental patient liberation," as it was first called, in part to a magazine called the *Madness Network News*. Initially published in the Bay Area in 1972, it was the first media published by and for "mental patients." (Its motto was "All the Fits that's News to Print.") Mental patients published the paper; they wrote about involuntary commitment and medication, they wrote about electroconvulsive therapy. The first antipsychiatry protests were held around then, in Berkeley and a few other American cities—which perhaps explains what Bob saw Bart participating in on TV. Some activists called their movement "madness pride" or "mad pride," reclaiming a slur in a manner not unlike other minority communities have done. Some call it the "c/s/x" movement, which stands for "consumer," "survivor," and "ex-patient." Some proudly call themselves "mad" or "crazy."

In 1978, an activist named Judi Chamberlin published one of the movement's most revered manifestos called *On Our Own: Patient-Controlled Alternatives to the Mental Health System*. Chamberlin had been diagnosed with a mental illness and found traditional psychiatric intervention unhelpful and even traumatic. She did recover, however, and she credited that recovery to an alternative mental health care facility she stayed at in Canada. Chamberlin and many other madness pride activists believe that people with "lived experience" should not only have a proverbial seat at the table when it comes to the creation of mental health care systems, but that such people are uniquely equipped to understand what constitutes the best treatment. A slogan Chamberlin sought to make famous was "Nothing about us without us."

In recent decades, people who've been psychiatrically diagnosed have organized, raised consciousness, and formed various organizations. Prominent lawsuits have limited the powers that states and families have to hold and medicate people. In some Western European countries especially, many "peer-led alternatives" have proliferated. There are safe houses, which are sometimes called "peer respites." There are peer-led support groups. Often of particular interest to people who've been diagnosed with schizophrenia are support groups facilitated by the Hearing Voices Network. These are nonclinical groups led by and for people who've heard voices or seen visions or had other "unusual or extreme" experiences. HVN began three decades ago and now has support groups in more than thirty countries. The organization points to research that's found that a majority of people who hear voices have never sought psychiatric help, which conflicts with the mainstream psychiatric view that voice hearing is a symptom of illness. Many HVN participants have previously had no forum in which to speak about these experiences without judgment or fear of repercussion.

Bob does reference hearing voices in his manuscript, though only once. It's one of the few lines I still can't quite make sense of. He describes telling a cop about MY VOICES, AND THE GUY, CHAIN MORON, WHO DISAPPEARED INTO THE CLOUDS. The only other mention of voices appears after he returned to La Casa Via: I WAS PUT BACK ON MEDICATION AND WAS CONSTANTLY ASKED IF I WAS HEARING VOICES: I WASNT:

Of course, Bob was likely discouraged from talking about voices or other unusual experiences in psychiatric settings, and in society generally. But many who've had such experiences reject psychiatric terms like "hallucination" or "delusion." Many understand them in the scheme of their own lives. There is strong evidence of a correlation between distressing voice hearing and the experience of early childhood trauma—sexual abuse especially. And many who hear voices do not find the experience distressing at all; some voice hearers regard their voices as guides or companions. I've met many voice hearers who've said they'd never want their voices to go away.

Some who participate in HVN groups come to understand their experiences spiritually—as Bob certainly did. In some cultures, both historically and at present, people who have such experiences aren't regarded as ill or abnormal or deficient, but rather as gifted.

In my experience, people who've been psychiatrically diagnosed feel a variety of ways about their diagnosis and about the field of psychiatry itself. Some who've been told they have schizophrenia agree with the diagnoses, and some feel that psychiatric medication has saved their lives. Others of the opposite persuasion champion for the abolition of psychiatry entirely. But many fall somewhere in between. Those who advocate for peer-led mental health care alternatives do not necessarily propose them at the exclusion of mainstream psychiatric methods like hospitalization or medication. The peer-led alternatives movement is mostly about empowering individuals to make sense of their own experiences and to figure out how to best care for themselves, especially given that distressing mental or emotional states are often periodic and have clear triggers.

These alternatives are not all that common in this country, nor well studied. Governmental health care spending is heavily biased toward biological inquiries—for example, exploring why psychiatric drugs work, or toward identifying genes correlated with a diagnosis like schizophrenia.

As some alternatives have taken root in this country in recent decades, others have worked to oppose them. Some groups feel that health care solutions that don't emphasize medication first and foremost are misguided—and even dangerous. Proponents of this position feel they are defending the "right to treatment" or "right to care." They might grapple with the fact that many who receive psychiatric diagnoses often dispute them, and that many patients resist taking psychiatric medications. Some psychiatrists conclude that patients who are resistant to treatment are exhibiting signs of "anosognosia," or "lack of insight" about their own disease. Psychiatric survivors I've spoken with find this charge—that a doctor might tell a patient she cannot understand herself, her own mind—to be especially offensive.

No two people I've interviewed or resources I've read about mental health care in America have felt the same way about what the right treatment should look like. But most everyone who follows these issues agree that the situation at present is quite grim. Many times through these years, I have waded into the seas of statistics having to do with people diagnosed with schizophrenia in this country and read how they've fared in recent decades: statistics concerning homelessness, with being incarcerated, with being shot and killed by police.

People diagnosed with schizophrenia today will live a life that is ten to twenty-five years shorter than the average. Many debate the cause of this "premature mortality," as I've sometimes read it phrased. Some blame the lack of sufficient funding for psychiatric hospitals and medications. Others, including some who've been compelled to take such medications, feel that they are contributing to the problem.

Though Bob complained about the drugs throughout his manuscript, toward its end, he offered his thoughts on them at greater length: SHRINKSD NEVER TRIED THE DRUGS THEY ADMINESTERED, AND THE DRUG COMPANIES BECAME RICH LEAGELY MAKING THIS SHIT: ALL THE DRUGS DID WAS BLUR MY VISION, RELAX MY SYSTEM, MAKE MY SPEACH LATHARGIC, AND STOP MY THINKING: AND ALL OF THEM WERE ADDICTIUNG WITH SIDE AFFECTS LIKE ANEL LEAKEGE, BRAIN HEMMERAGING, HEADACHES, VOMITING, HEART PROBLEMS, SEVERE ALLERGIC REACTIONS,

KIDNEY FAILER, STROKE, HEART DISEASE, DIABE-
TES, DIFICULTY BREATHING, CRAMPS, TIGHTNESS IN
CHESST, SWELLING OF THE MOUTH, SEIZERS, MENTLE
OR MOOD CHANGES, FEAVER, TREMORS, AND TROUBLKE
SLEEPING, WHEEZING, SHORTNESS IN BREATH, HIVES,
STOMACH CRAMPS, DIARHEA, NERVENESS, RASH, ITCH-
ING, JOINT PAIN, SWEALING, DIZZINESS, MUSCLE
PAIN,, YOU NAME IT, WHAT THE FUCK WAS I TAKING
THE SHIT FOR

Like Bob, many people who've been diagnosed with schizophrenia are smokers—by one estimate people who've been diagnosed are three times more likely to smoke. It's unclear what
causes this; some believe patients smoke to lessen the symptoms
of schizophrenia, others believe they do so to lessen the effect
of neuroleptic medications. Patients who consume neuroleptics
long-term also sometimes develop "tardive dyskinesia," tics or
tremors that mimic those of someone with Parkinson's disease.
But the long-term effects of consuming neuroleptic drugs are not
well studied. Drug companies tend to fund their own research;
trials often focus on looking at patients over a short-term period
and comparing their responses to those given a placebo.

Many activists and journalists have pointed to the financial
relationships between the pharmaceutical industry and much
academic research to do with psychiatric diagnoses and medications, as well as organizations that favor pharmaceutical
intervention at the exclusion of potentially less invasive and less
expensive alternatives. Some people who've chosen to quit neuroleptics often find that comes with an excruciating period of
withdrawal. Some feel that the addictiveness of these drugs isn't
sufficiently studied or communicated to patients. Those who
criticize neuroleptics sometimes call them "chemical straitjackets" or "chemical restraints" or just "tranquilizers."

Today, rates of schizophrenia diagnosis tend to be higher for
people of particular races and socioeconomic groups. A 2004
study found that black people were about four times as likely

to be diagnosed with schizophrenia as white people. Poor people are likelier than wealthier ones to be diagnosed. And outcomes for people who have been diagnosed tend to differ greatly according to a patient's means—which makes sense, given our lack of public support for mental health care, and our lack of affordable health care generally.

Many times I have contemplated how my uncle's story might have been different had he not been privileged to be white, or had he not come from a family able to afford private care and so much else.

I don't know if Gene understood how much of a difference his money likely made in his son's life. Once, I asked him what advice he'd give a parent in his position, hearing a diagnosis like "paranoid schizophrenia."

He wasn't eager to make generalizations, he said: "The disease is so varied."

He mentioned something I'd spoken about earlier, namely that a lot of people don't seem to understand what "schizophrenia" means. My grandfather alluded to his own limited understanding.

"You mentioned somebody that's 'paranoid schizophrenic,'" he said. That term didn't make him think of Bob, he said. "I think of the guys in San Francisco wandering around the street, hollering and fraternizing and so on. Talking to poles."

GOD HAD ANSWERED

Wendy got out of La Casa Via and got an apartment and a job in computers. She wanted Bob to come stay with her when he was released. She had met his mom, too, and his mom really liked her.

Dr. Widroe said it wasn't smart to do that and instead found space for Bob in a halfway house. Bob knew if he already started going against Widroe's recommendations, he'd be liable to undo all the progress he had made at La Casa Via, so he did as he was told.

He arrived at a big house in a small town. It was run by a woman named Dorothy. She was in her sixties and seemed nice. She cared for about ten people, mostly RETARDS, including two kids she'd adopted. Some were just old and seemed to have nowhere else to go.

Another one of the patients from La Casa Via, this dude David, went to the halfway house at the same time. Bob hadn't known David well inside—all he knew about why David had been at La Casa Via was that he'd gotten into some gunfight with his friends somewhere in some hills. All David seemed to want to do at the halfway house was play chess or stay in bed.

Bob, bored, started following Dorothy around. Dorothy worked hard. She spent all morning getting people up, getting them fed and bathed.

She didn't seem to mind Bob's company as she did dishes or made beds or sat down with a stack of bills and a checkbook. Dorothy, he learned, was cooler than she looked. She listened to Janis Joplin and was saving up to buy a Chevrolet Stingray.

After a few weeks, Bob asked her if she wouldn't mind if he sent for his guitar and amp and promised her he'd figure out a place to play that wasn't too loud. She agreed and let him plaster the walls of an abandoned shed on the property with egg crates to muffle the sound.

There was a hippie neighbor, a guy named Richard, who did odd jobs around Dorothy's property, helped her out. Richard was cool. Played the sax.

Soon Bob started following Richard around and helping him, too. He learned that Richard lived on a big piece of property nearby that he cared for.

He and Richard gardened. They rode down to dry riverbeds and collected boulders. They built rock walls and staircases and fire pits.

Bob liked Richard a lot. Richard liked to talk, but he also actually listened to what Bob had to say. He was interested to hear about some of the more intense shit that had happened in Bob's life, like being thrown into a cell alone in Herrick Hospital, or the flash of energy that'd touched him in the graveyard at Sunny Hills. Around Richard, Bob didn't feel stupid, like other people sometimes made him feel.

One night David commented on his friendship with Richard: "I don't know why you let him take advantage of you."

"What'd you say, man?" Bob asked.

"He doesn't pay you, does he? Has he ever offered to pay?" David said. "I'm not here to work for free."

"It's not like that," Bob said.

He preferred working with Richard to sitting around like David all day or watching Dorothy spoon-feed the drooling kids.

Bob knew Richard didn't like David, anyway.

Bob would never forget the first time Richard drove them in his rattling truck down the long dirt road to the place where he lived, which was called GAMBEDA.

Sunlight pounded through the pines and dusty air. Jays darted about and Bob could hear a creek warbling below.

There were a couple of old wooden buildings that looked like barns. Richard's wife, Jenny, came walking out of one, their baby boy on her hip.

They walked down toward where they were growing all kinds of fruits and vegetables. There was no electricity on the property, or running water, Richard explained, and they liked it that way. They lived off this garden, and that creek.

Berries ripened in the sun.

Big spiders waited in tangles of vines.

Bob said he couldn't believe that anybody actually got to live in a place this beautiful.

When his mom and Wendy came up to visit him some weeks later, he insisted they go down to Gambeda for a picnic.

Bob could tell Wendy was sad Bob was up here and not down with her living at her apartment. Bob couldn't help it, though, that this is where Widroe said it was best for him to be. He also maybe felt less for Wendy than he had at La Casa Via.

There was a doctor, Dr. P., who came by every few weeks and took Bob and David's blood pressure and maybe some blood, to make sure their medication levels were alright. One visit, for some reason, Dr. P. told Bob that Bob wasn't to have any more contact with his mom.

When his mom came up to visit again, this time with his little sister Debbie and her friend, Bob was told he had been kicked out of the halfway house. He called up his mom and asked if he could live with her. She said no. His dad said the same. Bob was allowed to stay only one more night with Dorothy.

In the kitchen he asked her what she would do.

"Pray tonight" was her answer. Dorothy was always praying; one of her adopted sons would sometimes drive a bunch of them fifty miles to a church in a van.

Bob didn't know how to pray.

He went to his room and lay on his bed, listening

to David snore. He looked at the ceiling and thought about that flash of energy at Sunny Hills. He wondered what the difference was between an alien and an angel. Both come from the sky, both demonstrate to us a level of existence that exceeds our own. So Bob tried to pray, for the first time in his life, murmuring to something called God.

In the morning he went downstairs. Richard was in the kitchen talking with Dorothy. Dorothy looked up from the stove and smiled.

"Bob," Richard said, "I was wondering if you want to come and live with me and Jenny."

Bob couldn't believe it. He hugged them both.

He packed up his stuff and Richard drove him over to Gambeda. Bob thought about how Richard's offer not only solved the problem of where he was going to live next; it did something much bigger. When Bob spoke to God, he risked hearing nothing back.

Instead, out of the dust and glimmer of outer space, GOD HAD ANSWERED.

Bob slept on Gambeda's earth and awoke with the giant sun.

Bob and Richard would head out and work. Sometimes other guys joined them. They hunted for deer and picked berries. They hung out in a sauna they'd constructed by the stream. The other guys were obsessed with sex; once they talked all about wife swapping.

After a day's work, when he was filthy with plaster or mud or goat shit from scraping pens at the farm up the way, he stripped naked and leapt into the freezing creek. The alpine runoff burned his legs and torso clean. He felt the strength in his thighs as he squatted to lean his blond hair back into the water, shut his eyes, and went all the way under. He emerged and stood there a long time drying.

For a whole hour he stood like this, experiencing every bit of his skin and hair.

As the weeks passed, Bob felt less and less guilty if he forgot to take his pills. The less he took them, in fact, the more he felt himself commune with nature. Days he didn't work with Richard he'd roam the massive property, naked, playing guitar.

As night set in, other hippies who lived around Gambeda would show up, like raccoons crawling out from behind a wood pile, sleeping babes in arm. The men threw bigger logs on the fire. They passed around a joint or maybe a jug of wine, if someone had something like that. Nobody had much. Far as Bob could tell, the only thing Richard and Jenny actually bought to eat that winter was honey.

Bob set his guitar on his naked thigh and strummed.

There was one beautiful new woman who had a fine voice. He wanted to walk with her into the dark woods and finally feel what it was like to have sex.

He smiled at her; she looked away.

He strummed more confidently now and sang as big as he could, and his and all their voices rose like the fire into the heavens above Gambeda.

Sundays, Richard drove to town for church. Bob usually waited in the truck or walked around. One time, as he waited for Richard, he found a pay phone. He called Wendy collect.

She had not long before mailed him a package with some jerky and a pillow. Her voice was shocked and lifted when she heard his, and sank when he told her he didn't love her anymore, and she shouldn't wait for him. He carefully returned the phone to its cradle.

He could have stayed there forever, and probably would have. One day, though, without warning, the guy who owned the property showed up and accused Richard of running a hippie commune.

Everybody had to go.

Richard said he was sorry.

Bob had bought a truck with some money he'd made from chopping down and selling a worm-infested apple tree. It was a '59 Chevy with a Thunderbird engine, a noisy bouncy jalopy. Bob filled its bed with his stuff. He said goodbye to Richard and to Jenny and their baby.

He drove away, watching them shrink in the mirror.

It felt good to be on the road again. Despite its appearance, the truck worked fine; just its speedometer was broken.

As he drove, he thought about Richard and Jenny, how much they'd given him. He thought about Dorothy, too. He thought about how many people she cared for. He thought about her adopted son driving people all that way to church.

He wondered where he should go next, and remembered a pamphlet he'd read for a community college up in Quincy called Feather River. He decided he'd drive to his dad's place and ask him to pay the tuition. He was so lost in thought he didn't notice the cop until he was right alongside him.

Bob rolled down his window and yelled, ::PACE ME, MY SPEEDOMETERS BROKEN::

The cop positioned his car in front of Bob's. For some long miles they drove like this, the cop and Bob, until the cop finally took an exit.

Bob couldn't believe that had worked.

His truck bumbled through his dad's neighborhood, one where everybody was a millionaire. He figured he and it must have looked pretty scuzzy.

His dad and Agnes did not seem pleased to see him. His dad said he could stay, but not for long. They agreed to pay for the community college up in Quincy.

Their carpeted stairs practically shuddered beneath his goat-shitty boots.

Before he left the Bay Area, he wanted to make a little money. One morning in the paper, he saw somebody who wanted a wall painted. For fifty bucks, Bob was that guy.

He drove down to some house in Piedmont.

The dude led him in. The inside was dark and sparse.

"This is it," he said, pointing at a wall. "Just paint it over."

The wall was orange, and on it was painted a three-foot-wide black seven-headed snake. It was exactly like the one photograph that'd been all over the news, Patty with a machine gun in a beret and fatigues.

Bob realized: this *was* the wall from that photograph.

He tried to act casual as he started to paint but wondered whether the SLA didn't have cameras in the house still.

He wondered if he was committing some sort of crime.

Or if the SLA would come after him.

With each glide of the roller, with each head of the snake he hid, he became more nervous and more nervous. At any moment someone might come and kidnap him—or worse. The roller circled and circled, and each stream it left was a mark of time passing, a sign that he was that much closer to being able to flee this place. He finally finished, got paid, and didn't mention the day or the job to a soul until he wrote the true story of his life.

Not long after, he moved up to Quincy. He enrolled in Feather River College and lived near campus with a roommate. The guy didn't even get up to say hello when Bob first arrived. Just sat there as Bob hauled his amp and his box of kitchen stuff, JUDGING THE HELL OUT OF ME.

Bob tried to tell him a bit about himself but the guy didn't seem to believe a word.

Bob was taking ceramics, mountaineering, and law, which he liked, and also typing (he DIDNT

HAVE A PRAYER IN TYPING). They went on some camping trips in his mountaineering class, and one time the teacher showed them this raccoon he'd made a pet and its babies.

What he liked most about Quincy was being near enough to the mountains to ski. He'd always been good at skiing. He loved most that feeling at the top of a run when he'd slide his tips about a foot out into the air above the inevitable descent. He would pause, take a breath, and feel the terror of gravity—and then let go. He loved going all the way to the top and exploring the backside. He loved to stop sometimes on a run, take off his hat, and listen to the white world.

It was about an hour and a half between Quincy and the resorts. He would sing to himself as he drove there or back. Or he would think about big things, perhaps because skiing made his soul soar.

Who was he?

Where was his life going?

Why was it that when his dad died someday they wouldn't burn his body on a boat, like the Vikings used to?

One night he awoke to the sound of a fight. His apartment was at the end of a road that was usually quiet. Listening from his bed, Bob reasoned it must have been a couple of drunks who'd happened to pick his street for their fight. He listened to them for a while.

Finally, he got out of bed, stepped into his boots, and walked over to open the front door. He stood on the mat and breathed the sharp air.

The snow radiated in the muffled moonlight.

Not a soul there.

It was weird.

He went back to bed.

He lay down and heard it again: definitely a fistfight.

He wondered whether he was hearing things, or whether he just couldn't tell where the sounds were coming from. He looked across the bedroom; his roommate was asleep.

Maybe it was a neighbor's television?

He decided to look one more time. Got up. Boots. Went to and opened the front door. And again, night and nothing else. He walked back to bed. Head on the pillow.

After a few moments, *thwack*.

Pause.

Thwack.

And something falling, like a stool. A stool falling onto a bar floor.

Thwack.

Thwackthwack.

He must have managed to fall asleep because before dawn he was awake again, and restless.

He dressed and walked toward downtown Quincy. The sun was emerging from behind a bluff of clouds as tall and white as a Sierra peak, casting everything gold.

Bob noticed a fat guy a ways down the road. The sun was becoming more and more inevitable, and the fat guy was turned to face it, too, and then, somehow, he walked into the sun and disappeared.

He was totally gone.

Was Bob still asleep?

Bob rolled a Bugler cigarette and kept walking. A cop came up alongside him and accused him of smoking a joint. Bob got so mad he threw the cigarette at the cop's chest, and soon he was being pushed up against a wall and frisked.

His face smashed into the cold brick, he told the cop about his voices, about the fistfight he had heard in the night, and about the guy he'd just seen who had walked into the sun.

THAT WAS SPOKEN LIKE A TRUE KING BOBBY: the cop said, and let him go.

How had the cop known his name?

A couple of days later, Bob was driving back from the slopes when another cop pulled him over on Highway 89. Bob asked the guy what the problem was—he hadn't been speeding—and the cop said he had snow on his back window.

Turned out that was illegal, something Bob hadn't known, which was how he'd gotten this fucking ticket. He could have tried calling his dad for help but was determined to work it out on his own.

He arrived at the Plumas County courthouse. He exhaled and stamped a cigarette into the slush. He leaned over to look at his face in the truck's side-view mirror.

He went inside and waited in a hall and then a courtroom and then they called his name. He was feeling crummy, sweating, had to hold on to a railing to steady himself when someone called his name and he walked up toward a judge.

The judge was an old dude, cleared his throat a lot.

"A thirty-dollar fine," the judge said, "or three days in jail." This guy didn't like Bob at all, he could tell.

"That doesn't seem right—"

"Excuse me, then, we can call it forty dollars."

"Whoa, man, wait, why—"

"Fifty, then."

Bob was getting pissed now. And the number kept going up—"Sixty! Seventy!"

Even a guy sitting there in the audience couldn't believe what he was hearing.

"Ninety, that's all! Next!"

Bob stood up and got out of there as fast as he could. He ran down the hall and down the courthouse steps.

He flung open the door of his truck.

Where was he going to get ninety bucks? His mom didn't have ninety bucks. His dad did, but fuck, he was so tired of the way it felt when he asked his dad for things.

He rolled and lit a shaking cigarette and swore aloud as he sped out of there.

It was a Thursday; he had class in the morning. That night at about eleven, he went outside and sat on the stoop.

It had begun to snow. He rolled a smoke.

He exhaled at the dark sky.

Patches of stars were visible through the clouds. Little bursts of wind bullied flocks of new snow around the driveway.

Maybe he should just drive his truck off a mountain.

He visualized how it would go: he'd aim off

some curve. He pictured the moment right before he pressed the pedal to the floor. Maybe it'd feel like the moment right before you take off down a ski slope. Floating, and then a jolt, and hopefully, then, he'd never have another thought again. People would blame his bad driving, or say he shouldn't have been driving in the first place. Or they'd just say it was an accident, which is what he'd want.

There'd be cops. Phone calls. His mom and his sisters would cry; that he didn't like picturing. At the funeral they'd be forced to be there in the same room, all of them. It wouldn't take long for everybody to forget about him entirely and for all record of him and what he'd gone through to disappear.

On some level, wouldn't they be glad he was dead?

For some minutes Bob had been noticing an especially big star. He became more aware of it and wondered what it was—a planet or satellite?—and as he did, it shot across the sky and froze in place directly above Quincy.

From it, a smaller capsule spiraled down.

They were back.

Bob grew afraid. He wasn't so much afraid of them, but for them, of what would happen to them if they went down into that little redneck town. Or anywhere else, for that matter.

How soon would the government show?

How soon would guns be drawn?

How soon would we be slaughtering God's angels like we slaughtered the Vietnamese?

Bob had begun to cry because there was nothing

he could do to stop it, the violence that was inevitable when the powerful crashed into the unknown.

All he could do was wish: Stop! Stop! Stop!

And the capsule did.

Bob couldn't believe it.

Get out of here! Bob's mind spoke to the capsule: I want to go with you, but it's not safe for you here.

The craft paused, as if listening to him. It then circled back up and the two melded together again and then shot back across the sky, and as it did, Bob was hit with his second jolt of energy.

He was down.

He found it was snowing on the carpet he was crawling across, but these hands and knees, they weren't his, he'd borrowed them for a little while from nothing and they'd be nothing again soon because he was barely a thing, Bob. Bob whose tears were raining on the carpet of snow. Bob whose blood was twinkling to a stop in his veins.

What is that sound?

That is the sound of God's angels. They are bathing him with their breath.

What are they telling him?

That all of the universe is inside of him, inside of his mind. They are telling him he is okay because God's angels are bathing him with their breath and telling him that all the galaxies are contained within his mind.

One of the aliens, she was his girlfriend

now, and she loved him more than anyone ever would.

How long was Bob suspended in this ecstasy, this ecstasy as thorough as death?

How long does it take to receive confirmation of the divine?

How, for the rest of his life, would anything ever feel so real?

Morning light splayed through the pine needles outside the window. Bob got up from the sofa. Looked at the clock on the stove. It was past nine. He was late for class. He didn't have time to change his clothes or eat or anything. Who knew when he last ate. He was out the door.

Campus was surprisingly dead. He went up to the building his class was supposed to be in and pulled on the handle. Locked.

He went to another building. Same thing.

What was going on here?

How long had the aliens had him?

Had something horrible happened in the world?

He sprinted back to his apartment.

His roommate was in the kitchen.

"Hey, man, what day is it?" Bob asked.

"Sunday."

His roommate looked at him weird.

Last he'd remembered, it'd been Thursday.

Three days, totally gone.

Three days he'd been with them.

His body was as tired as it had ever been in his life. His roommate was still looking at him weird as Bob stumbled to his bed.

He was on his back. His throat burned and his

eyes were watering and he had never felt more sick or spent in his life.

What had they done to him?

Another day gone.

The next morning, he rose again. Went to the living room. Dialed his dad. Agnes answered. Something about the way he sounded made her say, "We're coming to get you."

After a few hours, they would be there, his dad and Agnes, in a brand-new white Cadillac, an improbable vehicle to be carting around Bob, filthy Bob, raving Bob, Bob who never again would have to live in that dark apartment with that jerk of a vet: good riddance.

Soon he would be put back on the closed unit at La Casa Via. He would be forced back onto all the meds. Every day people would ask whether he was hearing voices; he wasn't. He also didn't want to talk to anyone, so for a while he didn't say a single word.

Six weeks he would stay at the hospital this time. He made some new friends, friends he'd have for years to come—this girl Becky and this dude Nick. He started going to this new therapy group, one he'd also attend for years, which was run by a woman named Bev.

Even though it looked like he was recovering, even when it looked like he was playing piano, or drinking coffee, or sitting on the patio smoking, he wasn't. He wouldn't tell anyone, but every day, all day, all he was focused on was forgetting that feeling, which had been, he knew, the most beautiful feeling in the universe.

Three Days

The first time I said the word "schizophrenia" in front of my grandma Marilyn, she got mad. It was maybe the maddest she'd ever been at me. Soon after, she mailed me a note saying that if I wrote that her son had *that,* I was "defaming" him. For a while afterward, I wondered whether her problem was with the word itself, or what she felt it implied about her son.

One afternoon, we sat in her backyard at a little white table beneath a lattice of grape leaves, and she read me letters that Bob had sent her back in the 1970s. She was the one most familiar with Bob's whereabouts throughout his twenties. He lived with her sporadically, sometimes in her house, sometimes paying rent to live in the apartment downstairs. I could still talk to her about Bob's mental health, I found, if I used euphemisms like "Bobby's problems."

She said she wasn't notified when Gene first took Bob to Herrick Hospital. Why Gene had taken Bob there, she didn't know. It was the biggest question. "To me, and to Bobby."

Bob had told her about what happened to him there. It was a story she'd heard many, many times, and it always made her very upset. "I just can't imagine Gene putting him through what he put that boy through," she said. "I just hate him for that. I just hate him."

She remembered going to see Bob at Herrick Hospital with her niece Jane. Once he started staying at the second hospital over in Walnut Creek, she'd go see him often, after work. She'd encourage her daughters to visit him, too.

She remembered the girlfriends I asked about, and the guys he played music with. She remembered times when people took advantage of him; she lamented how he was always handing people his money and things. She vaguely recalled something about a doctor who'd said Bob couldn't talk to her but didn't know what that was about. Marilyn's memory has been fading for years, and when she would nod that one thing or another was familiar, it was clear these recollections were as faint as the wind chimes on the other side of her tan house.

In letters to his mom, Bob wrote a lot about his religious convictions. He wrote about his various plans to get his life back on track—a job he wanted to get, a job he'd missed out on getting. He wrote a lot about how much he loved her. "'I didn't go to church last night,'" Marilyn read aloud from one of them, "'and I got to crying thinking of you.'"

Another he must have written after they'd had a fight: "Hope you can forgive and forget," he said. "I still think you're the greatest mom in the world and I love you."

Some of Bob's letters were written in a slanted cursive that was challenging to decipher. Others he'd written in boxy, careful capital letters. Some were postmarked from San Andreas, which was where both Dorothy's halfway house and GAMBEDA were. He signed them "Bob" and "Bobby" and "the hermit."

Her voice wobbled as she read.

Sometimes she wept.

Marilyn remembered the time she was at work and got a call from the community college up in Quincy. They said Bob was missing, that he'd been missing for days.

She didn't know what to do. She walked to a friend's desk, and they sat worrying.

Finally, the community college called back and said they'd found him. They said he was just sitting on his sofa.

She wondered, always, where he had been for those days.

Three days.

What had happened to him.

Marilyn was adamant that she believed her son about the aliens. Other relatives, mostly on her side of the family, made me promise that I'd include that they, too, believed Bob. Some detailed fantastic things they'd seen in their own lives, coincidences you could barely believe.

Other relatives felt that kind of talk disqualified him from being able to write truthfully about anything else.

Marilyn often spoke of her sense that Gene and Agnes were embarrassed by Bob. She pointed something out to me once, something I haven't been able to unnotice, though how she knew about it at all I am not sure.

In Gene and Agnes's front hall, just as you walked through their doors, which were very tall, there was a row of four sizable portraits.

They were of the four girls: my aunt Heather, my mom, and then each of Agnes's daughters. They'd been done in the mid-seventies in a style that looked like pencil, with thick cream-colored mats and matching brass frames. Each girl had been made to sit and smile in a similar manner, and each had her hair hanging long.

My mother is seventeen in hers and stunning. I'd always look at her and her sisters when I passed through those doors. Dozens of times I must have walked by them, putting on or taking off coats, giving brief hugs, and talking pleasant talk, those little white dogs yapping and running underfoot. Dozens of times I passed them and never noticed there wasn't one of Bob.

In the stack with her son's letters was a fragile piece of newspaper. It was a "Dear Abby" column from the mid-nineties that Marilyn had evidently clipped and saved for twenty years.

The woman writing to Abby explained that her son had been diagnosed with schizophrenia. "No one should have to endure what schizophrenia does to the mind, but worse is what society does to its sufferers," she had written. "If my son had been stricken with cancer, he would have received sympathy. Because he suffered instead from a mental illness that sometimes made him do weird things, he was treated as less than an animal by some people. Professionals in the judicial system called him a 'sorry piece of human flesh.'" This woman wrote that her son had often expressed a wish to fall asleep and never wake up, and that he had died in his sleep some years before.

Marilyn had underlined a part farther down in which the woman implored Abby to tell her readers to learn about mental illnesses, which affect one in four American families. "Look beyond the illness to the inner person. They need friends."

Marilyn patted this scrap of paper into my palm and looked me in the eyes.

It's a moment that comes to me often when I think about why it's so hard for some people to hear or say the word "schizophrenia."

LOUISIANA

He called it THE RETARD PROGRAM because that's what it was. His dad signed him up for it. It cost his dad $70 a week and he only earned $10 of that back.

He'd have to show up every day and they'd set him up with a box of cans and make him put on gloves. He'd take out one can, wipe a rag around the top, put it back. He'd take out another and wipe it and sometimes his glove would screech across the metal and give him the shivers.

He'd study the job listings in the paper each morning; he had to figure out something better. His strategy was he'd count the number of ads in different fields to figure out where the most openings were. That's how he decided on welding. He got his caseworker to help him apply for a government loan to pay for trade school.

Agnes would drop him down at the BART station and he'd ride over to Oakland. The loan paid for that fare, lunch at McDonald's, and the courses. He bought his own tools and hood, and wore goggles and gloves so heavy it felt like holding your hands underwater. About thirty other guys were there, some in their twenties like Bob, some older, some even older than his dad. They were a piratical bunch, slow-moving and ornery: X CONS, A HELLS ANGEL, LOWLIFES, LOOSERS, AND ME:

Their workroom was a large warehouse, low-lit but for the pops of ignition and raining sparks. Drains on the floor burped Oakland's shit and urine and mixed with the stench of agitated metals and burning things—canvas, hair, skin. Flatulence, too, and heavy, smoky breath and globs of sweat dotting the cement from the concentrated brows of the men, who, despite their various ages and races and former lives, were made uniform by their aprons and lowered hoods.

At lunch they'd eat from oily sacks and smoke outside in the sun, their jumpsuits unbuttoned and tied at the waist, revealing strong arms or flabby ones, and tattered undershirts, tattoos, dog tags, and crosses.

Often he ate his McDonald's alongside an ex-con named Wess, who wore a cross and talked mostly about Jesus. It was from Wess that Bob first learned that Jesus was going to be returning.

"It's all in the Bible, the future," Wess said.

"I never read it," Bob admitted.

Wess laughed real loud. "When you do, you'll see what I'm talking about," he replied. "I hadn't, either, before I went inside. Had time then. But now I do about whenever I can. Doesn't matter where you start, either."

He stood up wiping his hands on his jumpsuit.

He was beefy, Wess, with scars up and down his face like his face was snow and it had rained. Bob could tell if somebody threw a punch, Wess would do worse back.

"Or how about this," Wess said. "I'll steal you a copy from my church and you can see for yourself."

Wess started standing next to Bob in workshop and all day long yammered about Jesus. About how he'd felt before he met him. About how much better he felt now. Before, Wess had been involved with the largest LSD distributorship on the West Coast. He was on parole now and had millions he wasn't allowed to access until something happened with the courts. It was true Bob had no idea what he was going to do with his life. He had mental institutions on his permanent record now, so even with a welding certificate he might not get hired to work. The dream of being a musician seemed just that at this point, too. The idea of a book that told the future interested him, he admitted to Wess, who one day made good on his word and handed Bob a small Bible.

They had moved on to arc welding from gas welding, which meant if you forgot to put your hood down, you'd go blind. His dad and Agnes and his stepsisters probably couldn't stand the way he smelled, or the stories he told about class, or when he threw his charred laundry in with everybody else's. He'd come home each evening with a nose full of BIG BLACK BUGGERS and then sit in his room and read the book Wess had given him.

One day in class the guy next to him tapped his shoulder and said, "You're on fire."

Bob looked; he was.

He dropped to the floor and rolled in circles, his mask clanking and the flames groping at his groin.

The right leg of his jumpsuit was blackened and beneath he was fine, other than missing some hair. The other guys stood around laughing at him and helping him up and slapping his back. They had taken a liking to Bob once they heard his story, that he'd been kicked out of high school, that he'd been a logger, that he'd been in a band and lived up in the gold country. They knew the government was paying for his school but they didn't know why.

A couple of the other guys were Christians as well but of different stripes, and so in class there were fistfights all the time about Jesus. One of the black guys or Mexicans would say, "You don't know Jesus," and Wess would reply, "You wouldn't know Jesus if he bit you in the ass," and hoods would be up and gloves on the cement. Soon Bob found himself backing Wess in fights, because from what he was learning, Wess had things right.

Bob had been nervous at first to go to church. He wasn't sure what to do, but Wess told him to just copy what he did, said it'd be fine.

Every service Bob heard, every verse he read, every conversation with Wess, he became more certain he was doing the right thing.

He knew positively that God was real because

He had sent His angels to speak to him, twice now, and so this added bit about Jesus being His son wasn't such a leap, and the things Jesus said and stood for made sense to Bob. If the apocalypse did come—and who in their right mind can say it won't, eventually—better to be with this group that believed than with the sorry unbelievers, the kinds of people who cared less about heaven than they did about their cars and their real estate.

That's why one day Bob told Wess he'd like to be saved.

The next week, partway through service, the preacher had Bob come up to the front and get down on his knees next to a basin. As he spoke, the people swayed like weeds in a lake and the women began to moan.

As Bob's hair entered the water, their sound grew and as his ears went under he heard a rushing and their voices were muted behind the drone, and—oh that feeling. He had had friends along the way, people who'd guided him, people like Piute and Bart and Richard and now Wess. But Christ would be here now, always, within him, no matter what, even after his body died. They'd be together in heaven.

He emerged with open lungs and sucked in breath and the cacophony around him and felt DAMN GOOD ABOUT GOD.

After six months, they took exams in order to get their certificates. Wess pilfered a copy of the final from the offices and passed it around to the other guys, who didn't rat, and each memorized the answers in turn. They all passed easily, except the one guy who'd chosen to be honest.

Even if he hadn't cheated on his test, Bob knew that he still would have aced it.

There'd been this recruiter who visited them some weeks prior. He'd worn a hat and rubbed his chubby palms up and down his suspenders. He told them he was from Louisiana. They were all welcome to come down and apply to weld for his tugboat operation in Morgan City, he said. He walked down the filthy row of them, shaking their hands like they were something. Bob and Wess decided that was where they would go.

Wess got permission from his parole officer and Bob got permission from Dr. Widroe and his therapist Bev and filled a year's supply of his meds.

His dad gave him a couple hundred bucks and one of his cars, a Buick Electra convertible.

Before long, Wess and Bob were motoring south down 5, and then east on 10.

They crossed California's farmland and into Arizona's desert. Their ears popped and cleared and the air dried. Scrub and little else dotted the horizon. The road rose and fell.

Headlights in the opposing lanes lessened as night came on. They took turns, drove through and into the sunrise and New Mexico, stopping only for gas and jerky and coffee and cigarettes for Bob. Wess didn't smoke, he said, because he was a Christian. Bob hadn't heard before that Christians couldn't smoke.

The second night, both exhausted, they pulled

in to some small Texan town. They cruised down the tiny, unlit main street, peering out at the locked storefronts. They found some sort of park with a public bathroom. Not a soul about. They parked. Wess walked over to the bleachers to pray, and Bob, sitting in the car, nodded off.

They awoke to tapping on the windshield. A cop's knuckle. Wess was saying, "Good morning, Officer."

"What business you boys got here?"

"We're driving to Louisiana, welding work there," Wess said. "We're welders."

"California, comin' from?" He pointed at the Electra's plate.

"Yessir. Got into town too late," Wess said.

"No overnight parkin' here," the sheriff said.

"Sir," Wess said.

"Don' like folks comin' off the highway."

Wess was turning the key.

They were back on the road for a while, listening to their stomachs, when Wess broke the silence: "Sure am glad that cop didn't check the bathroom back there."

"Why?" Bob asked.

"Last night I went to throw all of your pills down the toilet after you fell asleep because you're a Christian now and you gotta stop taking that shit just like you gotta stop smoking that shit." He motioned to Bob's lit cigarette. "Anyway. Thing backed up and there's shit and pills all over the floor," Wess said, laughing.

Bob cracked up. He was a Christian now and

he knew he didn't need those pills or these smokes. He rolled down his window and threw the one in his hand into the desert and hooted and Wess shouted, "Praise the Lord!"

Bob took over driving somewhere between San Antonio and Houston. The air became more tropical and the traffic denser. The cars thinned out and again it was night.

Bob turned and glanced at Wess's snoring chin on his breastbone.

Imagine if Bob hadn't met Wess, how fucked he'd be.

Fleetwood Mac was playing on the radio as they finally crossed into Louisiana.

"Thunder only happens when it's raining," Stevie cooed to him.

Midday they pulled in to Morgan City, a town on the coast about an hour west of New Orleans. They got themselves set up in a motel for ten bucks and then headed out to find the wharf.

The air here was different, he noticed. In the Bay Area being near the ocean cooled things down but here it seemed to make them hotter. Creepers and vines grew up all the sides of the houses and moss like beards hung from the trees above. Bob had already sweated through his shirt. He noticed just about everyone here was either black or a redneck.

During their interview at the tugboat company, Wess and Bob showed the boss their welding school certificates. Everything seemed to be going fine. Then the interviewer took them down for a test.

186

"Well, boys," he said, and pointed, "we'd like to see what you can do. Run that sixty-footer up there uphill vertically."

Bob couldn't believe it: they had managed to name a weld he'd never been taught. Despite this, somehow Wess got up there and did it fine. How, Bob had no clue. Bob got up there and failed.

So this is where things started to go wrong.

The foreman felt bad for Bob and gave him a job assisting this seventy-year-old guy, Pappy, who hobbled around all day with a broom. It'd be ten hours a day for $4.60 an hour.

Bob would look up at the black guys with their hoods down and sparks flying and wanted another chance to prove he could weld but they wouldn't give it. Worse, everyone around the place loved Pappy because he'd worked there for about a thousand years. When he approached, people would stop their work and exclaim, "Hey, Pappy!"

Standing next to Pappy, who the fuck was Bob.

He and Wess rented a small house and at night they'd go home and strip to their underwear and sit in front of the one fan and eat soup or beans cold from a can; it was too hot to light the stove. Bob would tell Wess stories about Pappy and Wess would laugh and say, "Shit, man!"

They shared a wall with a woman Bob had seen a few times. Her husband was seldom home. She had black hair and big green eyes and was sweet and shy as a beat dog.

She always seemed to be home and would smile

at Bob from her window as he came back from work or from buying cigarettes at the corner store; he hadn't lasted long without them.

He imagined what it would be like to be alone with her, even though he wasn't supposed to think that way now, and all he knew about sex still came from what he'd seen at that Berkeley porno theater.

One evening there was a knock at their door. They'd just gotten home, him and Wess. Bob opened it and there she was, the neighbor.

"Hi, y'all," she said.

"Hi," Wess said. Bob tried to wave.

"I haven't introduced myself, I realized, which is rude."

"Not at all—" Wess said.

"Well, I made a mistake in frying up too much chicken just now. I wondered if you two were hungry, help me get rid of it." She smiled. Bob pictured her naked on a couch, like one of the women he'd seen on that moth-eaten screen.

"Sure, ma'am," Wess said. "That'd be great."

They followed her into the night. In her apartment, she passed between them—she was rail-thin—and set a dish of chicken on the little table. She told them to take a seat.

The chicken was the best thing he'd eaten in a long time. Afterward, they slapped mosquitoes, and she said a little about her life and asked them a lot about theirs. Her name was Bonnie; her husband worked the oil rigs. He'd found her up in Kentucky and brought her down here not too many months before.

The fact that they were from California

seemed to impress her. Wess had begun to talk about Jesus, and Bob reminded himself that was all he should be interested in talking about, too.

Then a truck pulled up out front and Bonnie exclaimed something to herself and stood. A big man got out and opened the gate and started up the walk. "What's going on here," he yelled at her.

"They're our neighbors—" she started to say to him.

"We're just talking about Jesus Christ," Bob interrupted.

Her husband paused. "That right?"

Wess started talking about Jesus now, and when Bob was able to catch them again—oh, the look in Bonnie's green eyes. That night and others, in bed in the same room as Wess, Bob had to focus on Jesus hard as ever to keep himself from thinking about Bonnie and what it would be like to run away with her, and Jesus wasn't always enough.

Sometimes when he fucked up at work it was on purpose, because he was bored, because he was doing fuck all following around Pappy for ten hours a day. He'd do something like make the grinder sound like a racecar. They'd let him do simple welds sometimes and sometimes he'd do them wrong on purpose.

One day the foreman called him over and pointed thirty feet up the tugboat they were working on.

"We're going to need you to get up there and finish her off," he said.

Bob looked up. He knew he couldn't use a grinder up that high without getting hurt. "Oh, yeah, *sure*," Bob said. "Why don't you bring me over a chair to stand on and I'll get that started."

"You get down to the office, then," the foreman said, "if you're not going to do what I said."

Bob didn't care if he was getting fired. He was happy to be out of there and away from Pappy. He walked into the boss's office with the supervisor a step behind him.

"Bob, what exactly is the problem here?"

What Bob said in reply nobody quite expected, not even Bob: "I got blessed in a church last night and God doesn't want me to work anymore."

See, he'd been walking around town the evening prior when he'd passed a little chapel lit up inside and filled with singing people. Bob walked in and disrupted the service with his screaming, his screaming about how there was no need for lawyers or doctors because God will provide. The singing stopped because of his screaming and soon he was at the altar and on his knees and bawling and the women and men and the preacher came up and put their hands on him and started their singing back up, louder like when crickets quiet at thunder but then come back stronger, and his screaming became sobbing, and they were shouting, shouting, "Bless you! Bless you!" After the service was through he stood around and told the story of how he'd come from California and had been baptized. He told them about his dad's important job. They were

190

all moved, he could tell, by the realness of his faith. They blessed him and sent him back into the night.

He told this story in the office as he was fired from the company for which he'd moved to Louisiana in the first place.

There was a silence, then the boss said, "Well, God bless you, then."

And Bob was free to leave.

He was putting some stuff away in the equipment shack when an old guy approached him and asked what had happened. Bob told the same story, especially the part about how he'd received word from God that he no longer needed to work.

"Tell me, what church is that?"

Bob explained to him where it was.

"Haven't heard of it in all my time here," he said, "and I lived here all my life."

"In Morgan City all your life, man, that right?" Bob asked.

"Yes, it is," the guy said.

Bob cracked up. Guy had lived here all his life and he didn't know where this chapel was.

He continued laughing as he walked off the docks and onto the street, away from the salty stench and seagull shit, laughed all the way to his and Wess's little house.

What a blessing it was, being fired. What a blessing it was, too, Morgan City. Morgan City where there were blacks and rednecks, sure, but blacks and rednecks it turned out had a lot more things right when it came to Jesus than those people back in Berkeley or anywhere else in California he'd lived. In Morgan City, you couldn't even buy a pack of cigarettes on a Sunday.

Bob started going to different churches every day, and when he wasn't in church, he'd walk around and proselytize. He still had the little Bible Wess had stolen for him and its pages were swollen with humidity.

He'd set out each morning usually at the same hour Wess headed for the wharf. He'd carry his guitar on his back.

He had no itinerary. He'd walk into town and find a street corner that suited him or else he'd walk through neighborhoods and smile at the older people on their porches or else he'd walk down roads and out of town.

Sometimes he'd squat on stoops and lean against buildings and play for whomever was in earshot—religious songs, his own songs, or songs about peace. People would toss change at his steel-toed boots or at least smile at him and he'd smile back and thank them and bless them. Sometimes small groups would gather.

Or sometimes he just walked.

Once, all the way out in the country, he came upon a lake, a lake just sitting there all by itself along the highway.

He had never seen anything so beautiful.

He knelt.

He touched his palms to it, and its touch made him cry.

GOD WAS SHOWING ME MIRRICLS I WOULD NEVER BE ABLE TO EXPLAIN:

He was sitting and playing guitar outside a HIGH CLASS restaurant one day when he decided to improvise a song about its history. The people who heard the song appreciated it so much, they asked him inside and offered him something to eat. Bob didn't have the heart to tell them that these days he wasn't eating anything but fruit, but he went inside anyway.

Inside it was freezing. There were leather booths separated by frosted glass. Chandeliers sparkled overhead. The kind of place where his dad would eat, not that his dad would ever have cause to go to Morgan City or anywhere else in Louisiana.

A man handed Bob a menu.

Bob thanked him for his kindness, but told them all he could accept was a glass of ice water. He thought on it for a second, and added, "And to use your phone."

The guy had a busboy lead him to the back where there was a pay phone between the bathroom doors. Bob asked him if he could bum some money to make a call. The only number he could think of off the top of his head was the house he'd grown up in, so he dialed there.

Some rings and then a voice. His sister Heather!

"It's Bob," he said.

"Hi, Bobby," she said, "where are you?"

"Louisiana," he said. "Just calling to say hi."

"Hi, Bobby."

"Oh, man, how are you?"

"I'm fine, Bobby, what do you need?"

"Just calling to say hi, man, I've been having some real incredible experiences, Heather, real incredible shit down here."

She told him she couldn't talk right now.

"Yeah, talk to you later, okay."

She was at Cal now, or she was just done with it, he couldn't remember. She was going to be an architect.

He set the phone back into its cradle.

He reentered the freezing dining room.

He felt like A SPIRITUYAL ALIEN ON ANOTHER PLANET and downed his glass of ice water.

One night he awoke to crying through the wall.

He sat up—Bonnie!

He ran barefoot outside into the yard. Her door was locked. There was no light on. He banged on it for a while and shouted her name and no one came.

He needed to get help. He ran out into the street and all the way to the nearest police station. There was one old guy in there watching a small television on his desk. His eyes opened only slightly more when he saw Bob. "Can I help you?"

Bob explained where he lived and what he'd heard and how he suspected Bonnie's husband could do worse than just hit her.

The guy didn't seem interested in helping.

Bob tried to protest and the cop told him he best be getting home. He glanced over the desk at Bob's bare feet. Bob didn't want to get locked up himself; all he was trying to do was help Bonnie.

Her house was still dark when he got back. He banged on her door some more and shouted her name. Maybe she really wasn't home. He went to his apartment. His feet stung. He sat on the sofa. Not long before, he and Bonnie had gone together to a bar. She had told him that she was running away from her husband. She was catching a bus back to her father's farm in Kentucky.

"Come with me, Bob," she had said, and leaned close to him. He smelled her and he wanted to, he wanted to be with Bonnie, and he wanted to live on a farm. She leaned over and as she did he watched her breasts fall and then, in her purse, he saw a rabbit.

Why was there a rabbit in her purse?

When had that happened?

Was she already gone?

He didn't sleep for long because something woke him.

He sat up in the dark.

Someone was in the apartment.

"Hey!" Bob stood up and they leapt on him—there were two or three of them. They had him on the floor and their knees and their fists were soaring through the air and landing on his gut and back and he was shocked from having been awoken but also because even a man who anticipates violence at all times is shocked when it actually arrives. He was so shocked that he didn't even really feel each blow as it landed with a *thwack thwack thwack*. He covered his face with his hands and curled on the floor.

"Shut the fuck up or I'll fucking kill you!" one of the dudes was screaming at him, so Bob stopped screaming or tried to stop screaming. "Shut the fuck up, you motherfucker!"

Bob was in a ball, his eyes closed.

Thwack thwack thwack.

"If you're not out of here by morning, we're going to fucking kill you," another voice said. "You hear me?"

Where was Wess? Were these guys here because of something Wess did? Was Wess really stupid enough to throw away everything and start dealing down here? What if the whole Louisiana thing hadn't had anything to do with welding at all?

"You hear me?!"

"Yes," Bob muttered.

"You better hear me," the guy yelled as the screen door slammed.

The chirring outside quieted.

And started back up again.

Bob stood up, slowly, and went to the window. There was no one out there. He'd have to deal with the whole Bonnie situation later. Or maybe the two situations were the same. Maybe these guys had gone over to Bonnie's first. He went to the kitchen and got a knife. He tucked it into his pocket, tugged his shirt over it, and pulled on his steel-toed boots.

There wasn't yet the anticipation of morning in the sky; he had time. He walked toward town. It seemed probable that the guys had gone to a bar to wait for daybreak, that they'd head from there to murder him and Wess. Was Wess already dead? Bob didn't have time to think about the possibilities; he had to find the guys before they found him.

He found only a handful of drunks on stools in the first dive, and in the second as well, and in both they all looked up at once like a den of possums. Bob backed out of each, muttering, "Excuse me, God bless. Excuse me, God bless."

He realized he didn't even know what the guys who were after him looked like, or whether they'd been two or three. They'd sounded young to him.

If only he'd been brave enough to peek through his hands.

He felt the blade's coolness against his belly as he walked.

He had never before imagined that he was going to be a murderer.

At some point he gave up finding them. He instead found a bush and sat down beneath it. Last thought he had before dozing off was maybe he should just kill himself before the guys did.

He awoke and got up and, looking at the house whose yard he was in, was glad no one had found him yet. Considering the position of the sun, it was late morning, maybe noon.

He started walking again. The skin beneath the knife was raw, and his entire body was sore.

He wondered where he should go. If he went back to the apartment, the guys would kill him. It was morning; they'd have already killed Wess.

The thought stopped him.

He was in the middle of the street.

He closed his eyes and tears fell into his beard.

Wess had been his best friend.

At least Wess had been a good Christian.

Bob was, too.

He reminded himself that if he died, he would join God, and Jesus, and now Wess. Hopefully Piute was saved when he was in the army.

It wasn't Bob's time, though, something was telling him.

It wasn't his time to die.

He still had business on earth.

He noticed a gun shop down the block and got an idea.

Inside, fans were spinning round and round and the man behind the register nodded morning.

"Can I use your phone?" Bob asked.

"Alright, then," the man said, and pointed to it.

Bob dialed 911. He explained to the woman where he was. Then he said: "Send cops. Or I'll kill everyone in here."

He thanked the clerk for letting him use his phone and walked back outside. He sat on the curb in the gun store's shade. Before long a squad car pulled up and the officer stepped out and walked over to Bob.

"What seems to be the matter, Bobby?" he asked.

Bob told the cop about the night he'd had, about the cry from the house next door, and the two or three guys who beat him and were going to kill him at dawn, and how he'd pursued them through the night with a knife but hadn't found them.

Bob needed the cop to believe him because he needed protection from the guys. He needed to go to jail.

That's why he told the cop: "I'm a SCHIZOID OFF A MEDS."

His heart was hammering as they cuffed him and set him in the backseat of the car. He slunk down and sang to himself. He wiggled his toes—they'd taken his boots when they'd taken his belt and his knife.

He was relieved that the guys could not kill him now.

In the cell he was given a meal and a newspaper. Wess was alive, it turned out, and came by to bring Bob some clothes. As he changed, he examined his whole body and could not find a single bruise.

The second night, the sheriff explained he and his wife were going to drive Bob up to the state mental hospital and reassured him that he wouldn't have a criminal record.

It was about three in the morning when they unlocked the cell and led him to the squad car. A few minutes into the drive, on the way out of town, the sheriff asked if Bob would duck down on the floor for a minute, so Bob did.

When neither the sheriff nor his wife were looking, Bob peered up. There was a crowd around the car, hundreds and hundreds of people awake in the middle of the night, all over the sidewalk and street. What was everybody doing out of bed? Were they there because of Bob?

On the highway the sheriff said, "It's okay now. You can sit up."

Bob was too afraid to ask him what had been going on.

They drove through the dark bayou for some time, silent at first, and then talking about God and joking around. The sheriff's wife seemed nice. At a gas station there was another sheriff's car waiting and they transferred Bob to it. Bob was relieved to find this sheriff was nice, too. This sheriff asked why Bob wanted to go to the mental institution.

"I just do," Bob said, afraid if he went into details, this sheriff would realize he was taking advantage of them for protection.

First thing that happened at the state hospital was a black orderly laughed in his face and said: "You'd *better* be crazy!"

Did this guy know Bob was lying?

"I'm working on getting well!" Bob said.

He was led to a table where some other guys on the closed ward were eating lunch. He looked at his own putrid tray.

He looked around.

He felt like he was going to puke.

They led him to his room. The guy on the next bed was as big and motionless as a fucking sea lion.

Bob had made a huge mistake.

He walked out to the front desk. He said he wasn't the person he had told them he was. That's when they cuffed him again and took him to prison.

At first, Bob tried to make the best of prison. It was sort of like a HEALTH SPA. There were basketball courts and the cafeteria was co-ed.

He'd twice now gotten away with taking two meals instead of just one and one time a woman sat behind him and braided his hair. He tried mostly to keep to himself, just sat in the corner and read his Bible. He didn't swallow the pills they gave him; didn't trust them.

And he was terrified of the guards. They were always angry, always yelling. Once this one kid went missing. Bob heard the guards beat him so bad he was hospitalized. Everybody speculated he was dead now.

Bob was stuck, stuck with no plan for how to get out, and for all he knew, it was only a matter of time before the guards went after him. He could barely sleep he was so worried.

One day during exercise time another inmate approached him. They had spoken before and Bob had told the guy about his fear he wouldn't survive long in this place.

"I'm planning some things," the guy now said.

It was pretty clear he was talking about breaking out. Bob had no choice, really.

He said he was in.

Whatever the plan was, it was happening tonight. Bob didn't get to know all the particulars because it was probably safer that way.

He must have fallen asleep because he awoke to his name. It seemed to be the afternoon. A guard was unlocking his door.

"Yeah?"

He was holding a parcel. "You have a visitor."

This was it.

They were going to kill him.

The guard said, "Come on, put these on."

He threw the parcel at Bob. Inside it were some clothes.

This was it. This was a setup. Bob had no choice but to do what the guy said. At least the street clothes would help him fit in, if he ever did escape.

He followed the guard down the hall.

"Who's here, man?" Bob asked.

"Your doctor."

Bob didn't have a doctor in Louisiana. The guy was definitely lying, he now knew.

This was it.

He was going to die.

He prayed under his breath.

His heart was still.

They opened a door—and behind it was his dad.

Bob was stunned, and then rushed to hug him.

"It's alright, okay." His dad shrunk from his hug. He whispered in Bob's ear: "I'm your doctor. Your parents sent me to get you home."

His dad was lying, Bob realized, MASKERADUNG AS A DOCTOR!

Bob couldn't believe it but had the sense to shut up and play along.

They waited around awhile and his dad signed things and eventually they walked out the prison's front doors.

They went to a hotel. He explained to Bob that he had interrupted a vacation he'd been on with Agnes in Hawaii.

He sat on one of the two beds and looked at his son.

The next morning they went to an airport and flew back to California. His dad dropped him off at La Casa Via. Bob later heard that Wess drove the car they'd had back west and moved up to Oregon, opened a huge Christian retreat up there.

Any Other Way

Agnes answered all of my questions clearly and without embellishment, our conversation sometimes feeling like a deposition. We were in the den. Behind her, the walls were lined with photographs of her daughters, all the grandchildren, books, and accolades about Gene. She sipped diet Pepsi from a crystal tumbler.

She told stories with little emotion: The time he called from jail and she had to go bail him out. The time he bicycled on the freeway. The time a neighbor called and he was walking around with a knife. Bob wasn't actually violent, she explained, "so when he would go around the neighborhood with a butcher knife, it was not to hurt anybody. It was for protection."

She said that he never actually lived with them, though he always would have been welcome. He may have stayed there a few times, but briefly. He seemed to prefer his own apartments. "He really wasn't all that comfortable, I don't think, around me," she said.

She and Gene were offended at the notion that they ever hid Bob from anyone.

"I don't go into a room and say, 'By the way, we have a schizophrenic son,'" she said, but if it came up in conversation, then she'd say, "Yes, he's disabled."

Agnes described how, when they'd had those portraits drawn, Bob's hair was very long and they wanted him to cut it. He refused. Later she did regret that they didn't just let him do it anyway. "So parents do make mistakes," she said.

Agnes had read that rural places were better for people with his diagnosis, which was why, sometime in the late seventies—he'd have been in his twenties—she'd begun driving through the country, looking for somewhere he could live. The property they eventually chose was in an area where, she felt, people wouldn't mind if he didn't mow or if he kept "junk" in the yard. There were no neighbors close by, so he could play his music as loud as he wanted. Later, some houses were built closer to his; people complained about the noise, and they had to soundproof the place. He could get to her and Gene, or they to him, in three hours.

The property they bought had a trailer on it at first (which he called the SHACK in his manuscript); after he'd tried it out for a year, they built the house I had visited (which he called the RANCH). They tried to get him to sleep in the bedroom, but he wanted his music equipment in there. They tried to give him new clothes, "but he really didn't like new things." They tried, too, to have a cleaning service come. She once wanted to give him one of those buttons that could summon help during an emergency, but he was very opposed to it; he said he spoke to his mom every day, so she'd know if something was wrong.

They bought him cars. They paid his vet bills and dental bills. They set up an "elaborate" trust for his care in the event of their deaths. They also gave him a fixed amount of money per month. She expressed that they were a bit embarrassed when he initially wanted to collect disability payments, though in time they understood his need for greater independence. The amount he got from the government never would have been enough to survive, however. "He'd be on the streets," she said, adding, "And that's what we've got on the streets."

Agnes was eager for me to understand that Gene and Bob did not have a tumultuous relationship. She emphasized how patient Gene always was with Bob, how he "never berated Bob for being sick or for not being able to get things done." Gene would call

Bob regularly; they'd go see him, too, as would other people on their side of the family. She contrasted that with those on his mother's side.

Agnes recalled seeing her husband get upset at Bob only a single time. They were at a restaurant and Bob ordered something "really expensive." Afterward, Gene apologized, she said.

She said that Bob, likewise, was very polite around them. She called her stepson "generous"; she praised his love of his family and his dogs, remarked upon what a "beautiful" skier he was.

Bob, too, had lost his temper in front of them only a single time that she could recall. He'd been down to visit for Christmas, in 2004, and there'd been a misunderstanding. She'd intended to give him half his annual money in one check and the other half soon after on his birthday. When he saw the amount was so much lower than usual, he thought he was being punished and got upset. He sent a letter not long after, apologizing. I AM VERY GRATEFUL FOR YOUR GENEROSITY AND KINDNES, AND REALLY, AT THIS POINTS, HAVENT THE FOGGIEST IDEA WHAT ID DO WITHOUT IT: he wrote. IM NOT GREEDY, AND DON'T NEED TO BE RICH IN THIS LIFE: I AM STUDDING RELIGIONS AND HAVE MADE SOME PRETTY REMARKABLE FINDINGS THAT IM SURE MANKIND WILL SOMEDAY REALIZE: BUT I ALSO LIVE A VERY PRIVATE LIFE AND VERY HAPPY WITH THE WAY ITS BEEN GOING: IM SORRY THAT HAP-PENED, AND WOULD LIKE TO FORGETT IT: THANKYOU SO MUCH FOR EVERYTHIONG!!!!!

In general Gene did not seem comfortable being asked such direct questions about his relationship with his son. Many of the stories Bob had written about the two of them weren't accurate, he said. He would never say a ham sandwich cost a fortune, or give a teenager a toy for a five-year-old. He had never taken his son to a barber and shaved his head and laughed at him—that, to him, sounded like something from a movie, and he wasn't balding back then, besides. He speculated that Marilyn's brother

Rollin, who went bald young, was the kind of person who'd play jokes like that.

I asked how he accounted for all the differences between their two memories, and he explained his sense that Bob often confused stories he'd heard from other people in the hospitals with things that had happened to him.

I asked whether it upset him that Bob had written these false and sometimes unflattering things about him.

"Well, he didn't say them to *me*," he said. "So I never heard them until now, with all of this."

In a letter to me, Agnes had included a section titled "Other things Gene did for Bob." There were the vacations at Tahoe cut short because of Bob's tutoring schedule. There was the time when Gene was teaching in Singapore and came back early because Bob was "in crisis." And of course there was the time when they'd been on a rare vacation in Hawaii and Gene had to fly to Louisiana.

It was a state hospital, not a prison, Gene said, though Bob had been facing indefinite involuntary commitment.

Gene got the call and flew all the way there. Then, he found, "they wouldn't let a parent in. Wouldn't let anybody in to see him. Wouldn't talk to me."

He had a little square briefcase with him, one like a pharmaceutical rep might carry. So he went to a different receptionist and pretended he worked for Roche. "I said I was a drug salesman and I wanted to see doctor so-and-so that was on the commitment papers. She took me right in."

Then he just didn't go away until that doctor gave him what he wanted, which was his son.

I asked how he knew to lie like that.

"I wasn't getting in any other way," he said, his voice as steady as ever.

THE FANNZE

He was walking back inside from the patio one day at La Casa Via when he saw this chick.

She was standing next to a doorway laughing about something, and as she laughed she tilted her neck back and Bob studied her throat and suddenly knew that all of the waiting for a girl like Lydia Treeantopolis had been for a reason and also that Christ's love wasn't going to stop him at all now. He looked at the clock; it wouldn't be long before visiting hours were up. He walked over.

"Hey," he said. He introduced himself.

She said her name was Nancy. She was the younger sister of one of the other patients.

They chatted.

When he made her laugh, again the throat emerged and he wanted to put his lips on it. He asked for her number and she gave it. He said he would call when he was out.

He was at La Casa Via about another four weeks this time. When he got out, his dad agreed to let him stay with them while he took another welding course; in the hospital he'd read about a pipeline up in Alaska they were building, work that paid $150 an hour.

Bob called Nancy. She came over and they had just gone down to his room when Agnes burst in and said it was inappropriate for him to have his door closed. She had daughters in this house.

He walked Nancy to the front door. Holding her hand, he said, "My stepmom, she doesn't get it, man."

"It's fine, Bob," Nancy said.

He finished the welding course and got a job at a trucking company and moved in with his mom. It was only about a week before they'd fought so much, she'd thrown his stuff on the curb while he was at work. She called him there, pissed.

"That your wife?" another guy asked.

"Nah," Bob said, "that's my mom," and they both cracked up.

So he found an apartment in Oakland and moved in there.

Nancy lived with her parents in a suburb called Pittsburg about thirty minutes north. He'd drive up every night he could and take her out. They'd park and drink beers and kiss but he could never get her into the backseat. At ten on the dot he'd have to drop her back home. He'd then race back down to Oakland to start his night shift. He was driving about two hundred miles a day all told, and didn't have time to sleep, or eat much, and his meds were spacing him out.

:::::

210

One time, she came to his place. He wondered if he was finally going to have sex.

He shut the door behind them and walked her to his waterbed. They fell over on top of one another. He slowly reached up to feel her soft underwear, riding the waves beneath them, and removed his shirt and pants. She, too, was almost naked now and they moved and moved with tongues and hands. He slid his fingers into her.

His dick, though, was limp.

The meds.

They continued kissing for a while, but then slowed. Then stopped. He wondered what was going on inside Nancy's head. His face was hot.

"Why don't we take a shower?" she whispered.

He said that sounded like a good idea.

They stood in the small stream of water together.

Bob hugged her waist and leaned his head on her dripping shoulders.

It occurred to him that he was in love.

She took him to meet her parents. Her dad was in the living room, watching a game. Nancy sat next to Bob and said to her dad, "Bob works at the pier, for the Matson Truck Company."

Her dad nodded without looking away from the screen.

"And what does your father do?" he asked Bob.

Bob explained about his dad.

"Why didn't you follow him into that?" Nancy's dad asked.

There was a pause.

Nancy looked at Bob.

"I'm not sure," he said.

Not long after, his boss fired him without explanation.

He drove up through the foggy night to get Nancy. He didn't say right away why he was upset. He parked overlooking where the Sacramento and Joaquin rivers flowed into the bay. The reeds were dark and jagged like spears.

"I got fired," he said.

"I think we should break up" was her reply.

He didn't say anything back.

"Bob?" she asked.

He took his hand off her thigh.

"Why?" he finally asked.

"You're too good, you're too good for me" was the only explanation she gave, no matter how many times he asked, no matter how hard he hit the steering wheel with his hands. At some point she muttered that she wanted to go home and so he started the car and sped to her house. He would never see her house again; he would never see her again. He felt like he was going to puke, and he slammed on the brakes, and she got out and she ran, she ran up the steps to her house and slammed her door and he sped away into the foggy night muttering, "You're too good for me," and then yelling it, "You're too good for me!" He had never had as much *nothing* as this—no family, no job, no Nancy.

He thought about this Jewish chick Judy he knew from his therapy group. Judy had trouble making friends and had then fucked this new kid in the group called SUNSHINE BOY, which wasn't allowed, and after Bev had cussed Judy out, JUDY KILLED HERSELF THAT WEEK. He thought about this other kid in the group, a Cal student whose complicated sentences pissed Bob off. One time Bob had threatened to fight him and HE KILLED HIMSELF THAT WEEK. He thought, too, about this ex-boxer Ronnie he'd known at La Casa Via. One day during music class Ronnie had realized that nobody loved him and hanged himself in the bathroom while in the next room everyone sang.

Somehow Bob made it until the morning and then drove to La Casa Via.

While he was in this time, the only thing interesting that happened was he met a guy from Afghanistan whose father was a millionaire.

The guy was sweet, but he loved war. He told Bob all about the things America had done to his country; Bob had no idea. Years later, Bob suspected that it had been right then and there the idea of flying planes into the World Trade Center originated. Bob later saw the guy on the cover of *Time*. He didn't read the article, though, so he didn't know why.

When he got out, he moved in with his mom, who'd gotten all his stuff out of his apartment in Oakland and sold his truck. He got a job at an ARCO gas station in Walnut Creek.

He got to wear a shirt that had his name on it. He filled cars with gas, read tire pressure, squeegeed windshields. He made about $200 a week.

Soon enough, things were going great at

the job, so he decided to make things more interesting. Bob would often hear the mechanics whistle as the high school girls from up the way passed morning and afternoon. One day he decided to approach two of them.

"Hey there," he said to the girls.

"Hey," one said, and then looked at her friend.

"Do you know any musicians in the area?" was what he thought to ask. "I'm a musician and am looking to form a band."

Turned out they did.

That's how he met this guy Mike. They called their band the Third Rail and started playing parties all over. Before long a crew of about fifteen high schoolers started coming around the gas station to hang out with Bob every afternoon. He became especially good friends with Mike and this kid Scott. Two girls were into him, including a chick named Helen.

One night Helen invited him to a party.

In the dark she started to kiss him and said she wanted to leave. He drove her to his mom's place. In his bed she took off all of her clothes. He didn't have sex with her that night, though; he didn't know her well enough.

In the morning she followed him upstairs to the kitchen and he introduced her to his mom.

"Good to meet you, Helen," his mom said.

He was glad his mom was being so cool. He dropped Helen off a few blocks away from school and started worrying as soon as he got to work. Should he have had sex with her, in case she didn't want to see him again? Or what if he never got to see her again because her parents got mad at her for staying at his house?

He was surprised when she again walked up to the gas station later that afternoon. He told her his fears and she said there was nothing to worry about; her parents thought she'd stayed with a friend. She asked him to go to another party that night in the hills. He ended up with seven high schoolers in his car, and bought them beer, which they all drank sitting around a bonfire.

He looked over at Helen's face in the firelight and she pinched his side. She laughed at every joke he made. Maybe she really liked Bob. Or maybe she was just acting her age.

She stayed over again that night.

Soon enough, he was HAVING SEX WITH HELEN EVERYWHERE:

Summer had begun, and there were county fairs to go to, and Great America theme park, too. Bob loved roller coasters. He loved especially that anticipatory moment after you click-click-clicked to an apex, that moment when you hung there before the descent.

Bob never thought that high schoolers would like him let alone make him feel popular. During this time, when he hung out with them and was in the band and had his chick Helen and his friends Mike and Scott, he felt KIND OF LIKE THE FANNZE ON HAPPY DAYS:

The only thing that wasn't going great was his therapy group with Bev. He still went to it once a week; each session cost his dad sixty bucks. Bev herself was starting to piss Bob off. She'd argue that he should be saving all the money he was spending on booze and hanging around with Helen and the high schoolers. Maybe his dad was getting her to say those things.

High school started up again, so Helen and Mike and Scott and the others weren't around as much and September grew hot. The pine trees popped with seeds. He and Mike had a fight about the band. Mike's mom had offered them $10,000 of her own money to open for the band War when they played the Concord Pavilion.

Bob knew from all his time around veterans that vets really respected War. He didn't think the Third Rail was ready for a gig that big, and told Mike as much.

"Picture it, man, all those people laughing at us!" Bob argued.

Mike wouldn't listen. Mike just wanted fame.

Bob stormed out. Never spoke to Mike again. He heard from someone that Mike ended up playing the show without him. That made him even more upset; now everybody would think he was a loser.

At the gas station, one of the high schoolers had gotten in a fight with his girlfriend, had swung at her with a metal pipe. Bob had been trusted now to run shifts by himself, do bank runs and payroll, but this kid got arrested, and when Bob called his boss to explain what happened, he got fired. A few days later Bob called begging for his job back and got it on the contingency that he never let any of the kids come around again.

There was a gas crisis and the station had to enforce a $2-per-customer limit. A big line of cars stretched out of the lot and down the street and sometimes all the way around the corner. He'd spend all day racing around, arguing with people about the maximum.

One long-line afternoon, when Bob was the only one working the station, a guy got out of his car and pulled out a gun.

Bob dropped his arms by his sides.

The guy filled his tank all the way, got back in, turned on the engine, and pulled off the lot.

Bob spotted a cop across the boulevard and yelled, "He stole gas!"

Cops caught the guy later, he heard.

One time these three girls, other high schoolers, insisted Bob go with them to the drive-in. That was weird. Then, weirder, they only wanted to talk during the movie, talk all about how Helen was cheating on him.

Bob answered that that was absurd. They'd never cheat on each other. He'd gone to Disneyland not long before with his mom and Debbie, and because Helen's parents hadn't let her go, he'd taken Scott along. On Tom Sawyer's Island, Scott had raised his eyebrows at some chicks who passed and said that he and Bob should make a play for them. Bob had reminded Scott that he was in love with Helen.

Ever since the girls had told him about those rumors, though, he hadn't been able to think of anything else.

Soon after, he and Helen went to a crowded house party. There were kids everywhere, some of them shooting up and snorting shit, and right away he lost her in the dark.

He wandered from room to room calling her name.

Finally, he found her. She was passed out on a bed, mouth open, legs splayed. She wouldn't wake up. He hoisted her limp body up and into the car. He drove home through the dawn.

Helen would never cheat on him; they were in love.

The gas station was being sold and so he started working as a janitor at a couple of community colleges, a gig he got thanks to a government program called CETA. He and the other guys got along. They washed windows. They gardened and painted and fixed plumbing.

They had keys to everything—the basketball courts, the pools. There was one room with cadavers, and floating inside a jar on a counter was some dead dude's dick. Bob's favorite was the planetarium. He loved to go in there and turn on the whole universe.

Bob liked the janitors, especially this dude GARRY. One time he and Garry were cleaning an Olympic-sized pool, and it was so hot out they jumped in together, buck-naked and laughing.

Garry was a veteran. He'd bought his own house and went down to the military base to eat on weekends.

Helen had been acting weird. Also he'd run into this chick Maggie—whose dad Mac used to date his mom—and they'd hung out a couple times. Maggie had huge boobs now and she and Bob had fun joking around.

Helen was pissed, even though she still came

over every day after school and had sex with
Bob at his mom's house.

One time after work he went to Garry's and Garry
showed him his bird. It was a big parrot that had
cost hundreds. Garry was teaching it to talk.

Maybe, Bob thought, the parrot would cheer
Helen up.

He convinced Garry to let him borrow it and
put the big gold cage on his front seat. He
drove over to the high school and waited in the
lot until he saw people filing out.

He saw her.

He got the cage and walked up to where Helen
was sitting with a group of kids.

"Hey, Helen," he said, "look!" and he took
off the pillowcase.

"What is that?" she asked.

"It's a bird," he said, "Garry's. It talks,
man."

"What's it doing here?"

"I thought it'd cheer you up!" he said. "It's
a pretty smart creature."

She said she'd call him later.

His mom kicked him out again and he moved in
with this woman named Pam whom he'd met at
a community college. Her place was over in
Antioch. She had four kids by four fathers and
a fifth on the way by her boyfriend Bill, a
nice black guy who played basketball.

One day Bob got a call. "I understand you
know my daughter, Helen?" the guy on the phone
asked.

"Yeah, Helen, yeah."

"You realize my daughter is sixteen years old."

"Yeah, man."

"You ever see my daughter again, we will call the police."

Bob got scared and hung up the phone. He decided to drive to Scott's to ask him whether it was true they could lock him up. It hadn't occurred to him that having sex with Helen was illegal.

On his way over to Scott's, he saw a woman who looked like Helen walking with a dude dressed like a marine.

He slowed and then pulled over.

It was her.

Helen looked shocked to see Bob. She walked over to his car and the marine followed. The marine leaned over and shook Bob's hand through the window. Guy was a little too smooth for Bob's liking.

Something was wrong with Helen and he demanded to know what.

She eventually admitted the SMOOTH MARINE had given her weed. Bob reminded her he hadn't even let her smoke when he took her to a Led Zeppelin concert.

Some stupid things were said and Bob split.

That night when she called, he demanded to know if she'd fucked the marine.

"We're just friends," she said. "He was having a hard day. He's AWOL."

All Bob could picture was how little space

there'd been between the marine's pant leg and Helen's skirt.

He screamed at her to admit it, admit it.

"I'm sorry," she finally whispered.

He threw the phone at the wall.

That was it.

That was it with women.

He felt the waves inside him growing larger and larger.

He burst into the kitchen and Pam was sitting there. She asked him what was wrong. He sobbed that he had just broken up with Helen. She had him sit at the kitchen table.

They talked for a long while about Helen, and Nancy, too, whom for some reason Bob was thinking about again, perhaps because Nancy never would have done anything like get high and fuck some sleazy marine named Steve.

Bob felt himself calming down some as Pam told him the various stories of the men who'd fathered her soon-to-be-five children.

"Look at my life," Pam said. "You think I expected this?"

Bob hadn't thought of it that way.

"Hey, you know what?" Pam said. "We should throw a party. That'll get your mind off of it."

It was a great idea.

Pam rolled hundreds of joints and set them in bowls and they bought a ton of beer and soon there were kids sitting and talking and smoking and drinking and laughing and fucking on everything. Bob was in the garage playing guitar and chatting up a bunch of chicks. He and some other dudes had recently recorded a song, a song about saying goodbye.

He had played the track for Helen and she hadn't believed it was him. He was proving that it was him to these chicks when the cops walked in.

"It's my house," Bob answered the light in his face.

"Whose alcohol is this?" one of the officers asked.

"Mine, it's all mine, man," Bob said, "I'm twenty-three." Bob explained the beers were just being kept cold out here in the garage.

Pam came out, too, and got rid of the cops somehow. The party carried on.

After that Bob went to Pam with all his problems, like when this new guy who was working with the janitors showed up at work real fucked up. He couldn't talk, let alone drive a truck, and his eyes were rolling around like gumballs. A couple of guys put the guy into Bob's car and he took him home to Pam, who somehow figured out the guy needed to get back to Philadelphia, where he was from. Then there was this chick who was so fucked up she'd sucked off an entire basketball team; Bob brought her home and Pam drove her to get her stomach pumped.

At one point he got another call. It was that chick Maggie with the huge boobs. She said her mom was trying to have her committed.

"Why?" Bob asked. Maggie got straight A's.

She didn't know, she said.

Bob asked Pam if Maggie could stay with them and Pam said sure, for a little while. Bob and

Pam went over and got her enrolled at the high school. Bob figured that was better than her having a mental institution record, and Maggie was able to help Pam out with the kids.

One day he came home and Pam was crying behind a closed bathroom door. Her four children were wandering around in the dark house like strays.

Bob turned on a light in the kitchen.

He knocked and asked her what had happened.

She'd had a MISS CARRIAGE, she said.

Not long before, Bill had confessed to Bob that he was cheating on Pam. Now, leaning against the door, Bob nearly told Pam about what Bill had said. But he didn't.

When she later found out about the cheating, and that Bob had known, she kicked Bob out and he never saw her again. He often thought back to her, though, and about how she'd done that nice thing for him, helped him throw a party when a girl broke his heart.

He thought, too, about the best night he'd had with the janitors. A bunch of them had driven up to a rental place at Tahoe and smoked a bunch of weed, sat up all night talking and laughing about shit.

On his drive back down, he stopped at an inn. He sat down at the bar.

Two blond women who worked there started chatting him up.

One asked what he did and when he said he was a musician her eyes brightened. She explained they were looking for a guitarist to play in their house band!

He went out to his car and came back with his guitar and amp. He played for them and they smiled. If he took the gig, he could stay for free upstairs, they said, and eat all his meals at the bar. He told them he'd have to think about it.

He walked out to the lot.

He drove away.

Why, he wasn't sure.

He'd wonder for years after whether not taking that gig had been a big mistake.

What a Shame

When Bob mailed me his original manuscript, he included with it a letter that Agnes had written him not long before. He explained in a postscript immediately after his story's final line why she had written it. He had been down visiting after his dad had hip surgery. He and Agnes had gotten to talking about Bob's relationship with Gene, and Bob had said something that had really PISSED HER OFF.

In her letter, Agnes asked Bob to imagine being a "young father" who'd just been through a "bitter divorce" and was working hard to raise his "much-loved son." Then a "tragedy" struck: the boy developed schizophrenia. She discussed how hard the young father had to work to afford care and tutors and such for the boy, which were all very expensive. All this, and the boy continually "bad mouths" his father. "He seems to forget how sick he was," she wrote, asking if he remembered going through the neighborhood with a knife. "Does he remember all the voices that he couldn't control?"

She implored him to imagine how frustrated he would feel if he were that young father. "How hurt that the boy shows no compassion about what you were going through and how hard you tried to do the right things."

And yet, her letter concludes, "the boy feels so bitter that he 'can barely talk to the dude.' What a shame."

It's always seemed to me like this must have been part of why he decided to write down his own story of his life. (I'd note that, on his cover page, he called himself a boy.)

In his manuscript's final pages, he addressed a series of key topics, ones he understandably wished to be heard on and believed.

He discussed again Herrick Hospital, the traumas he experienced there, and Dr. G. He speculated that Dr. G. had experimented on him, adding that he'd seen something about experiments performed on mental patients once on TV.

He repeated, as he did whenever he brought up Herrick, that it was his dad who took him there. I THINK HE WAS A FOOL FOR WHAT HE DID, he wrote, adding his dad should have SUED THE SYSTEM.

HE MUST HAVE REALLY HATED ME, HIS ONLY SON, WHO HE DOESNT GIVE A SHIT ABOUT, BUT INSTEADS LISTENS TO DOCTORS WHO HAVE A BIG REPUTAYION INSTEAD OF THE TRUTH:

He noted the conflicted way he felt about his father: I'M GRATEFULL, YET RESENTFUL AT THE SAME TIME

Despite how negatively he felt about the medications, and despite the fact that nobody was really watching him once he moved up north, he kept taking them.

He certainly did so in part to maintain the equilibrium he'd reached with his dad and Agnes, which he called THE PROGRAM.

It's often the case that people prescribed psychiatric medications have a complicated relationship with them. This was true for Bob, who in one line mentioned that they did have some benefit: IF I GO OFF MY MEDS I MIGHT THINK HASTFULLY, AND THERES NO NEED TO DO THAT THE DRUGS SUCK, BUT TO HONOR MY FATHER I TAKRE THEM:

THE SERVICE

The Mormon temple in Oakland was just about the most majestic building he had ever seen. It stood atop a hill, all white except for its spires, which were gold and severe and looked like they could stab the underside of heaven. Palms fringed the drive. Bob walked up, taking it all in.

Inside, it was pretty quiet. He told a man he found that he was a big believer in God and had been looking for a CHURCH WITH A HIGHER CALIBER:

They showed him a video about Joseph Smith's life and handed him a copy of *The Book of Mormon*. He agreed that Joseph Smith must have been a prophet, ALTHOUGH I WASSNT SURE ABOUT THE ANGLE HE TALKED TO SO I TOOK IT FOR GRANIT: He told them he was in.

He started going to the Mormon Hall in Berkeley and was baptized again there. His dad and Agnes both showed up for the ceremony. He moved out of his mom's and in with some Mormons. One was this guy named Dave, and the other was a teacher who, it turned out, once had Helen in his class. He did a thing for money on the side that he let Bob get in on:

227

he bought these beautiful photos of wildlife—wolves and eagles—had them framed, and then sold them to businesspeople on their lunch breaks in Oakland. Bob thought it was a great idea, and even bought one for himself.

There was a second coincidence that involved Helen. It turned out she worked at an ice cream parlor just down the street.

He went down to see her once.

He left, embarrassed.

He was unsure why he'd gone.

There were a few women at church who wanted to date him but he wasn't interested. One kept bothering him to take her places, so he took her to his apartment and she fell in love with Dave. Guess he had MADE A MATCH:

He scored another job cleaning at a trucking company and a dentist's office in Oakland. He'd never realized how big a city Oakland actually was, and he always got freaked out and lost driving there.

He hadn't had this new custodial gig long when he was accused of drinking on the job by the owner of the trucking company. He told his boss he had seen a bottle of whiskey in the trucking company owner's office, but he hadn't touched it. Bob, now a Mormon, didn't drink. It didn't matter, and he was fired.

Next he got hired by the city of Martinez to be a code enforcer. He'd lied on the application, said he was a veteran. He figured he'd been around enough vets, he could pass as one.

His job was to drive around in a truck that said "City of Martinez" on the door and make sure people didn't have fences that were over three feet tall or trailers in their front yards or boats in their driveways.

Being around people had gotten exhausting, so he moved out of the Mormons' place and into an apartment complex in Lafayette.

One night at church, they said they were going to baptize a bunch of dead people and told Bob he had to leave—it was for elders only. Bob argued he should stay. He said there wasn't any way he could know God better than he already did, and they agreed.

They all went back to this room that Bob could tell was sacred. Some of the people put on gowns. He knelt and they dunked his head underwater and said some name. Then they did it again.

Sixty-five times in all they dunked his head underwater, saying names each time of the people they were saving.

At one point the name they said was "Joseph Smith."

Bob, his head all wet, stopped and laughed. "Joseph Smith?" he repeated.

The other guys laughed, too.

Must have been a different Joseph Smith.

He started seeing a girl he met at church, a woman who was tall and weird. It turned out she had a boyfriend back east, but she let Bob take her for a walk on a beach over in Marin, and then to his apartment. They started kissing and Bob heard a loud bang. Later, he learned that it had been one of his neighbors blowing out his own brains.

He and the tall girl and some other Mormons sang Christmas carols, and another time he took her to a movie. Then she told him she was leaving, had to go back to Boston. He drove over to her dorm to give her a bracelet and say goodbye. Somebody must have seen his City of Martinez truck on the freeway far from where it was supposed to be, and Bob got in trouble. He could sense he'd need to be moving on from this job soon, anyway; his boss had recently brought up Bob's service, asked how it'd been in 'Nam.

One afternoon not long after, he spotted a big boat parked in some driveway. He got out of his truck and was writing up a citation when a guy walked out of the house, asked Bob what was going on. Bob explained it, and the guy said: "Would you mind repeating all that into a tape recorder?"

Bob didn't know what that meant and refused.

Back at city hall, his boss called him into his office. The mayor was there, too, and they said Bob was being fired because he GOT PERSONALL WITH SOMEONE:

"Who?" Bob demanded to know.

They wouldn't say.

That was the end of his time as a code enforcer. Bob didn't like being an authority figure, anyway, and didn't like that he was living a lie.

Now he had no income and nowhere to stay.

He decided to GO BACK TO LA CASA VIA AND GETME HEAD BACK TOGETHJER:

:::::

One day, on the open unit, he was sitting strumming his twelve-string when a guy walked by and complimented his song.

"I'm working on a song," the guy said.

Bob said great.

The guy went and got his guitar and together they sat on the patio.

The song the guy played was called "The Gambler."

"That was the coolest thing I've ever heard," Bob said.

The guy explained he drove around in a van and his name was Kenny Rogers. They shook hands. Unfortunately, Kenny wasn't on the same ward or in Bob's same therapy group, but they still managed to hang out and jam a few times. Bob asked Kenny once why he was at the hospital, and all he said was "I feel rotten."

Bob met Kenny's wife and daughter when they came to visit. Then, right before Kenny was released, he played a concert for everybody in the dayroom, and even asked if Bob wanted to play bass on one number.

Playing with Kenny Rogers, Bob found, was FUNNER THAN HELL. Bob was grinning big and one patient burst into tears, she was so moved by their song. Bob later found out that Kenny asked his doctor whether Bob could come with him on tour but he'd said no.

Kenny got out and Bob never saw him again.

Bob stayed at La Casa Via just two more weeks this time. Something weird was Bob recognized someone from back at Herrick—the bearded black guy who'd called a code green on him the first time he was hospitalized.

His friends Becky and Nick were there again this time. They spent so many hours together, smoking, drinking coffee, laughing. They'd go on field trips together, too. They laughed especially when people out in the world would stare at them.

I THOUGHT IT WAS FUNNY TO WATCH THE PUBLIC TRY TO FIGURE US OUT:

He moved into his mom's downstairs apartment and got a job detailing expensive cars through the Mormon church. Then one day he saw an ironworking job listed in the paper that paid $12 an hour. Bob told the guy he was a welder and got hired.

The first morning he had to be all the way in San Francisco at 6:30 a.m. sharp. They taught him how to do something called rodbusting, where he had to lay rebar and then tie it off, over and over, fast as possible. By the afternoon his hands were raw.

He commuted each day across the Bay Bridge into the City, and then, when his Honda Civic died, on a bike, rain or fog or sun. He worked as fast as he could, trying to get everything done before the other guys came through and poured concrete. The work was hard, and the other rodbusters were mean.

He built a parking lot at San Francisco International Airport. He built a big cement silo down in Davenport, which was the toughest job he'd ever had, standing on a moving platform, tying and tying, while the cement came pouring right behind. He slept for a week after that job, and then got a bill for his busted car that was about as much as he'd made.

He did a high-rise next, hung there over the edge, hundreds of feet up, drilling holes with a thirty-pound drill and putting in clips where windows would be, and then someday, he figured, people who worked in offices, people like his dad, would stand there and not even realize how amazing a thing it was, a skyscraper. His boss told him he better be careful up that high—you spit and hit somebody in the head, you could kill them, and then wind up in jail for the rest of your life.

Bob didn't mind his boss. Guy was a Christian, at least. Sometimes he and Bob would talk at lunch. Bob told him how he'd been kicked out of Berkeley High for fighting with a guy who wanted to charge him a dime to piss.

"I would have whipped it out and pissed all over him," his boss replied, which was just about the funniest thing Bob had ever heard.

A given job might last a couple of days or even a couple of weeks. After, his back would ache and palms would bleed and he'd sleep in the dark for a week.

When Bob wasn't working, he'd bum around at this pizza joint in Berkeley called La Val's. He'd eat pizza and drink beer, which seemed fine given that he wasn't hanging out as much with the Mormons these days.

One time this black dude was standing out in front of La Val's, yelling at everybody walking past: "What time is it, motherfucka? What time is it?"

Bob bought him a slice and they played a game of chess.

After that, whenever the guy saw him—his name was Jude, and he was crazy and a genius—he'd yell, "The king! The king!"

Another night this Davy Crockett-looking guy named Jim was reading poetry and Bob started playing some Hendrix on the pizzeria's busted piano. The combo was a hit, and they scheduled a show together, even got it listed in the paper.

Problem was Jim liked to drink and he always got Bob real drunk, too.

The night of their supposed show, they got so drunk they themselves forgot to show up, and instead Bob was splayed in front of La Val's puking into a storm drain.

He spat into his beard.

He rested his head on the pavement.

It just so happened that right across the street from the ironworkers' office was an air force recruitment office. Bob was getting pretty tired of how much rodbusting was kicking his ass and walked into the recruitment office one day, just to see.

As with the Mormons, the first thing they had him do was watch a video. Bob told the recruiter he was a certified welder, which the recruiter said was great. Then Bob said he had a MENTLE RECORD.

"Just don't mention it," the recruiter said, and set Bob up to take an examination to see if he was air force material. A few days later he passed WITH FLYING COLORS.

He told his dad about the idea and his dad
said it sounded good.

It was 1979. He was twenty-five. Finally, after
so much transience and being made to do so many
insignificant things, he had found his calling.
It made sense, actually, that what he'd end up
doing was being in THE SERVICE.

He imagined what it'd be like, coming home,
standing on his dad's doorstep, saluting him.

He imagined how proud his mom would be.

He fantasized about stopping by La Casa Via
for a visit, or even going down to Herrick to
find Dr. G., to show him what an impressive
person he'd managed to become.

Maybe someday he would have a wife waiting
for him back at the base, maybe in Germany,
where he'd work as a nuclear missile technician—
they'd given him an option of becoming either
that or a radio dispatcher in Alaska. He figured
missiles sounded cooler.

He imagined walking in the door to his own
house each evening. He imagined holding his
wife through the night. He imagined waking up to
coffee and his shined shoes waiting by the door.

The wife he pictured was sometimes Helen in
her ice cream parlor uniform or sometimes Nancy.
Only occasionally was it Wendy or Bonnie with
her green eyes and the rabbit in her purse. He
still thought about Lydia Treeantopolis, too.

He wondered what she looked like now.

Before he left for the service, he met up
with his friend Becky, who was out of La Casa
Via, too. She was doing good. They went on a
date to the City, to this light show called the

Laserium. They stood outside beforehand and smoked a joint.

Inside, it was dark and then the lights began.

Becky by his side, his eyes were full of shit nobody actually understands.

The shaky military plane landed on a gray Texas day.

He ducked and ran across the tarmac behind the line of fellow recruits, deafened by the engines, his hair whipping about. He didn't mind that they were going to cut it off.

He'd heard about all the other things he'd be getting this first week in the air force: clothes, boots, new glasses. Six weeks of hard work and he would be on his way to a salary, stability, and a level of respect he had never before commanded.

Week zero of basic military training, new trainees were up at 4:45 a.m. and running. The chilly San Antonio morning woke up his mind and he kept up easily with his group of new recruits, called his flight, despite the blisters his new boots were giving him and the odd feeling that generally came with adjusting to living without his meds. He had figured they would piss-test him and so hadn't taken a single pill with him to Texas.

After running came inspection, class, drills, inspection, running, class, drills.

Everywhere they went they had to march, which Bob was great at, just like he'd been great at traffic boys as a kid and at hiking on those expeditions down in the Sierras.

Bob felt sharp in the service. There was no time to think and also no need. A command would be yelled at him—they all called him by his last name—and he would yell back, "Sir, reported as ordered!"

The mess hall was beautiful and kind of terrifying. Bob was overwhelmed by how many guys would all be in there at once. The thousands of recruits, their tens of thousands of fingers clutching thousands of trays, their tens of thousands of piles of mashed potatoes. All their uniforms, all their newly buzzed heads.

He only got twenty minutes for each meal, and most of that was spent in line. By the time he actually sat down with his own food, he only had time to chug and slurp and then had to be back in a line again.

Lights were out by nine and Bob slept hard.

They'd been told of the various jobs they could choose to have at Lackland. Bob listed his preferences as :::MEDIC::PILAT:::ASTRONAUGHT: AND SOUL SAVER::: He also volunteered to be his flight's chaplain when they got to attend religious services on Sundays.

The next day, his training officer told Bob, "Son, I have a sorry feeling in my heart that you are not going to make it."

Bob asked him why.

"There are no soul savers in the service."

This guy didn't know that no one tells a chaplain he can't bring souls to God.

When Sunday came, Bob marched his flight to the chapel doors. They were locked, which was weird. "Wait here," he told them.

He found a side entrance.

He passed several little rooms, and he could see people of different faiths worshipping, each in their own way.

Nobody seemed to respond to him being there. He wondered if he was invisible.

Now he heard a QUIRE singing, a lot of them, coming from somewhere.

He thought, WOW, WHERE THE HELL I HAVE I BEENM::

He went back outside.

His flight was all still waiting. He told them church was over; it was time to go.

During inspection later, this guy wouldn't give Bob a hanger. "Where's mine?" Bob asked. Lots of people heard. Bob asked two more times: "Where is mine? Where is mine?" Guy must have been embarrassed when Bob reported him for what he'd done.

Then someone called out his last name.

"Pack your things!" he was told.

He stuffed his junk into a duffel and followed behind.

They walked to a big building.

He was admitted to the psych ward.

How familiar: syringes.

How familiar: drugs.

How familiar not being taken seriously when he complained that somebody stole all his money the afternoon of his arrival, which someone had. He told them exactly what happened and nobody did anything about it.

Soon he settled down.

He got to know the dining options and what the place had to offer—arts and crafts, piano, volleyball, movies. A guy even showed up one night and told jokes so funny Bob was rolling on the floor.

Group therapy was even more intense than usual, given how many of these guys had been in 'Nam, how many of them saw bombs falling when they closed their eyes. One guy had been a pilot, talked about all the napalm he'd dropped, talked about how horrible he felt all the time. IT WAS OUR JOB TO HELP HIM, ORDERS YOU KNOW:

One day there was word, on the ward, that a highly classified mission had just rescued an important family from Iran; they made them all move beds to accommodate the family when they arrived. An elite squad showed up, too. Guys were all too cocky for Bob's liking.

He ate in the cafeteria alongside the son of the Iranian family a few times. He enjoyed their conversations. Bob advised him that they should melt the entire Middle East and make freeways and buildings and castles from glass.

He had lately been thinking a lot about Helen. One night he went down to the phone and gave her a call.

A man's voice answered, sounded mad.

Bob dropped the phone.

He leaned against the wall, breathing hard.

Why had he done that.

On Christmas morning, there were presents beneath the tree in the dayroom.

A general was there. He admired the presents and the tree. He stuck out his hand and Bob shook it. After the presents were all open, Bob sat down at the piano, banging out what carols he could conjure.

He and then others sang.

They sang about angels.

They sang about peace on earth and mercy mild.

They sang about God and sinners reconciled.

They had him back on Prolixin, but he was still getting ANCY. He started pushing them to let him out. They asked if he wanted to stay in the air force or split, walking him down a hallway where about three hundred girls were changing, all stripped down to their bras. He understandably couldn't help but look at them. Some big sergeant screamed at him, "What are you looking at, boy?"

What kind of head games were they playing with him?

He had to get out of there.

A few days later in group, someone called his last name and said he was free. He got to keep his medals and his chaplain's cross and silver bars. They gave him his pay and a piece of paper saying he'd been discharged honorably.

He sat on the bus on his way to the airport. The comedian whose jokes Bob had so enjoyed was on the bus, too, and asked Bob if he could borrow money for his flight. Bob knew he'd probably never see the guy again but gave him fifty bucks anyway. Figured what the hell;

everybody in the service was always screwing over everybody else, far as he could tell.

When he called his dad to explain he wasn't staying in the service, his dad sounded DICUSTED LIKE YOU COULDNT BELIEVE:

He told Bob to just take a taxi from the airport, said he'd pay.

They didn't want him staying with them for long. It was his birthday a couple days later anyway, so his dad paid for a month's rent at a board-and-care place in the City.

He dropped by an ironworkers' meeting to see if they'd still let him work. They asked where he'd been.

"The air force," he replied.

"What for, asshole?" they asked.

He said he didn't know.

The Story
of Annadonia

At the end of his manuscript, Bob discussed society as a whole. He talked about materialism and sexual promiscuity. He talked about violence. He discussed the tremendous population of people who would not, by his estimation, make it into heaven.

The imperfect nature of society is a common theme in some of his other writings, which I've since collected. Some years ago, for example, he wrote a short story on a computer, which he'd periodically mail to various relatives. It's called "The Story of Ishmall."

It's about two societies—Ishmall and Annadonia—between whom power is imbalanced. Annadonia is strong and Ishmall is weak. Annadonia seizes control of Ishmall. Annadonia grows even stronger and Ishmall even weaker. Perceiving this inequality but not remembering its root, the people of Annadonia decide that the people of Ishmall must be lazy. They give the people of Ishmall medications that make them even lazier. The people of Annadonia compel the people of Ishmall to take these medications against their will.

"The people of Ishmall were considered a burden by the rest of the world," Bob wrote, "and the world thought they should be compassionate and humane and feed the remaining people of Ishmall until they died a natural death. Six hundred years later there was no record or remembrance of the people or country of Ishmall."

But the story of the people of Ishmall does not end there. There is, in this story, an afterlife, and the people of Ishmall, who are very religious, get to be with God and have control over the souls of the dead people of Annadonia.

"Ishmall had won!" it ended.

He then signed it "Uncle Bob."

For a long time, I tried to figure out what it meant, the phrase psychotic paranoid schizophrenic. Whenever I tried to grasp it, it would fall through my fingers like wet sand.

In trying to figure that question out, I actually ended up thinking a lot about its converse. Through these years, I've wondered what they're supposed to mean, words like "normal," "sane."

I've thought about this desire that we—whom you might call the people of Annadonia—have to define abnormality. I have thought about our desire to think about schizophrenia as if it is caused by a pathogen; to segregate people who are told they have it; to ignore or doubt, on principle, what they have to say.

I've thought about our desire to imprison a man within that diagnosis, to let it become who he is, and to cast a shadow of silence around the subject.

I think it's because we are very afraid. None of us knows for sure what's in store for us inside our own brains.

What an especially frightening word it is, too. For years now I've said it to all kinds of people—not only people I'm talking to about Bob but friends, strangers, people I've just met, people who've asked, "What do you do?" and then, "What's the book about?"

For years I've watched how they react.

How their voices, their eyes, fall.

People sometimes ask questions that give away all kinds of things they think about my uncle because he had that diagnosis. That he was less than human somehow. A monster. A liar.

Some people are familiar with the word. They usually begin to tell me about their job or about someone they know—an

244

estranged aunt, which second cousin—or their own parent or own child. Occasionally, people will start telling me about themselves, about experiences they've had, diagnoses they've received.

But most people, I've found, are more like I was before Bob mailed me his manuscript. When I say "schizophrenia" to them, I don't know what kinds of images flash through their minds.

Sometimes people ask me how working on Bob's project has changed me; it's a question that makes me laugh, it's got so many answers. I'll give one: before, I was someone who didn't much care about schizophrenia or what it did or didn't mean, or what did or didn't happen to people told they had it. I must have believed such questions didn't much affect me. Now I know that the way in which my uncle was treated betrays something very wrong with our society, something that hurts us all.

Some people would have preferred that I hadn't gone this route, that I'd never agreed to help get Bob's story out there. Some of my own relationships have been irrevocably damaged because I made this choice. But in a sense I felt I had no choice. By the time everything was out in the open, I had come to believe that going forward with the project was the right thing to do. That I would tell what I have seen, painful and shocking as the details often are.

Through these years, I have read about societies that don't segregate and punish differences in this way. Ones where people like Bob are able to live lives not so greatly dependent upon figures like their parents, lives not so marked by the looming threat of incarceration and death, lives less marred by the violence and judgments of a hegemony who—generously—just haven't been taught any better.

I've read about what people in other places and times have thought about people like Bob, which is to say, people who experienced things that others determined were unbelievable, people who believed those experiences with conviction. Occasionally, such people were able to convince others of their truth. I've contemplated the lives of so many prophets, so many artists and revolutionaries and martyrs.

All the time I encounter news articles about the "suspected link" between some quality and another—"creativity" and "madness," for example—and to me it's kind of obvious that some of us have heads that are likelier to wander beyond the supposed edges of reality, whatever that is.

And that we are each just ourselves: whatever we inherited, whatever we've become along the way.

I have also chewed endlessly on the irony that my uncle's manuscript boldly stated his variously hateful views, and yet he also yearned for greater understanding and harmony between all kinds of people. I've often thought about how, in that note he sent along with his manuscript back in 2009, he implored me to not worry about his beliefs.

He did believe peace was possible; I don't think he would have bothered to write the whole thing down if he didn't believe that.

Because I don't think he did it for himself.

He was living for the next life, not this one.

I think he did it because he knew it was wrong, that someday humanity might be deprived of any historical record of the people of Ishmall.

TABBACO ROAD

The board-and-care place was like a hive that never slept. The front-desk guy had raised his eyebrows at Bob's bike, saying it'd probably get stolen.

Bob's roommate was a Chinese guy, and the tub in their room was broken. Bob tried to sleep but only watched the shadows move as people—porno stars and LUNITICS—walked up and down the halls all night long. He grasped his sheet and wondered why he'd ever left the service.

The next day he called and made an appointment for later that week with Dr. Widroe.

He hung up and called right back, saying he'd actually like to come in now. He rode his bike over and they put him on the open unit.

I FELT ONCE MORE:::AT HOME::

While he was at La Casa Via this time, he remembered a conversation he'd had with Scott before he'd gone into the air force. Bob had been trying to convince Scott to go with him.

He had ridden over to Scott's house early one morning to talk about it. Scott must have had a party the previous night and there were about six drunks all sprawled around on the sofas and floor.

Bob stepped over blinking bodies, trying to find Scott.

He opened one bedroom door and saw a woman in a bed—it was Helen!

She was asleep and there was a man beside her—Steve the marine!

Just the thought of that moment, when he saw Helen, saw that marine's hairy arm, Bob felt fury rush through him.

I GUESS IT WAS HARD GETTING OVER JER

Bob talked to Scott about the air force, but Scott said they wouldn't take him because he had flat feet.

Bob consoled himself with the fact that he had gotten one chick's number while he was in the air force base hospital. He also remembered this fat chick named Leanne, whom he'd met through Scott. Before he'd left for the service, he'd promised to marry her if she lost a hundred pounds.

Now that he was back, he worried about running into her; what if she'd kept her end of the bargain? Did he want to marry her? He worried about what to tell her now, BUT I WAS NUTS ANYWAYS SO WHAT THE HELL:

There was this one quiet guy back at La Casa Via he'd met whose name was Dan. Bob had asked Dan what he was into, and Dan had said all he did these days was play chess. Bob had asked what he did for money, and Dan had said he got checks from the government. Didn't have to do anything, just got paid for being nuts.

Bob brought it up with his doctor, Widroe, asked if he could get money like that. Widroe said he'd get back to him in a few days.

Problem was, he didn't have time: the ironworkers needed to know if he was coming back. He was basically broke.

A few more days passed and he still hadn't heard from Widroe.

He knew his opportunity to rejoin the ironworkers had passed, so he had to get disability payments now.

He went back to La Casa Via and said to the receptionist that he needed to see Widroe right away.

She told him to have a seat and he did.

Just then, the door opened and in walked the last person on earth Bob would ever have expected to see: Dr. G.!

He couldn't believe it. His insides were like fire ants in a Louisiana backyard drowning in a flash flood of piss.

"Hey," Bob stood and stammered to Dr. G.

Dr. G. half-nodded at him and muttered, "Hello," moving so briskly he was already gone.

The motherfucker didn't even remember him.

It was outrageous. To contemplate how severely this man, this one man, had fucked up Bob's life—locking him in that cell, practically killing him, giving him a mental record that followed him around for the entire rest of his life. How many jobs had he tried to get. Just recently, to name a few, he'd tried to become a Fuller Brush man, and a door-to-door knife salesman, and a firefighter—none of them would let him apply if he had a mental record. It had been practically the first question on the firefighting application: "Have you ever had a mental illness or been in a mental health facility?" And Bob was just one person! How many other people had he seen at Herrick, on the floor, tears pouring from their faces, begging to not be injected, then being so drugged they couldn't even stand!

He thought about how stupid his dad was for taking him there. He thought about how hard his mom had been fucked over by the divorce. He thought about his dad's second family. His dad's second family, they were HAPPIER THAN SHIT: He'd said things like this in front of his dad before and his dad would always get pissed, say it was the best medical care available and he worked DAMN HARD to take care of him and nobody would ever ask him about his mental record SO I DONT WANT TO HEAR ANYMORE ABOUT IT:

Dr. G.

That old devil fuck.

Finally, Widroe came out and he followed him to his office. Widroe introduced him to a social worker. Bob signed all kinds of paperwork.

When it was done, Widroe smiled at him and said ::YOUR ON TABBACO ROAD NOW:::

Bob didn't get what that meant.

As he was passing again through the waiting room—attempting to process this idea that he'd never have to work and could never work again— he saw someone else unexpected. It was the lady in the neck brace, the one who might have been Lydia Treeantopolis's sister. She had a kid with her, a little boy.

Again she took his picture.
WHO WAS SHE:

Some weeks later he opened an envelope and
stood looking at his first check.

He was on Prolixin and lithium and Artane. He
went to his therapy group once a week. He saw
Widroe every two.

He had no idea what he was going to do with
his life now.

He enrolled in an art class and a math class at
a community college. In one of the classrooms,
there was a really hard math problem that
someone had written on the board. For about
three weeks he argued with whoever was around
about the answer. THERE ANSWER WAS WRONG, AND SO
WAS MINE, AND THE ANSWER WAS NEVER ASTBALISHED
BY ANYONE, SO I DROPPED OUT:

He rode his bike.

He visited Joanne and Leanne and some other
fat girls. They were all escorts. They sat
around in a hot tub.

He went back to the pizza joint La Val's and
of course there was that crazy genius Jude,
who again shouted, "The king! The king!" Bob
laughed. They sat at the piano and Bob played
and he and Jude sang and jumped around as loud
as they could, their beers sloshing on the
floor.

He moved in with his mom. She must have felt
sorry for him. She took him golfing; he was too
drugged to care. She took him on a sailboat
with some old dude; he was too drugged to care.
He didn't have anything to say to anybody.

His friend Garry showed up one day and Bob turned him on to Prolixin.

Come morning Garry wasn't breathing.

Bob picked up the phone and an ambulance came.

Real cool medicine, thought Bob.

He was on the closed ward.

He was on the open one.

He moved in with this dude he met in his therapy group.

They smoked weed, and they got in touch with Garry. Garry, it turned out, had been up north somewhere, panning for gold; it was a miracle they'd managed to find him.

They shared stories about the service. Garry had been to Korea. Garry had gotten to go all the way to Korea; Bob hadn't gotten to do shit.

He hung out with another chick he met at La Casa Via. They went down and rode horses in Half Moon Bay. He told her he wanted something to wake up his mind.

They went into the City and scored some crank and drove over to Berkeley and up to Tilden Park. He had been there as a kid. He had been there as a teenager on a field trip from Herrick Hospital.

The cop car didn't look like a cop car.

On his asphalt bed Bob awoke to handcuffs on his wrists.

Later his dad got them to drop the felony charge. All he had to do was six months of drug court.

He was on the closed unit.

He was on the open one.

His black roommate punched him in the mouth.

The next morning, while the guy was still asleep, he smashed him in the head with his guitar and screamed: "I pop you in the head, motherfucker!"

Everybody heard.

A few weeks later, when they were both on the open ward, Bob's parents came to visit and so did that guy's. Bob looked at him, shot him a look that said don't try anything. It worked; he left Bob alone, and treated him LIKE GOLD the rest of the time they were there.

This other kid tried to fight Bob but Bob just stood there and yelled "nurse" and the kid got tackled. Later the kid was kicked out for good, because he was too violent.

He moved in with his mom.

He did crank with Joanne and the escorts.

He met up with his friend Nick, from La Casa Via, and they drank beers. Nick had a friend of his come over, too, this famous black musician. They drank and drank and drank.

"Hey," Bob's tongue flapped, "we should call Becky."

"Yes, yes," Nick said. "We should call Becky."

Bob and Nick and the famous black musician fell onto their feet and they ripped apart Nick's room until they found a book where he'd written down her number and on the wall was the phone. Bob got his finger in there and dialed the whole thing out.

"It's ringing!" he screamed, and Nick leapt up and down.

"Hello?" a woman's voice answered.

"Becky!"

"I'm her sister," the woman said.

"Becky around?" he said as carefully as he could. "It's her friend Bob."

"Becky is dead," said Becky's sister. "She jumped off the Golden Gate Bridge."

He was on the closed unit.

He told Widroe he wanted to go up to Napa, to the state hospital there. He wanted to just stay there for the rest of his life.

He thought often about what it'd be like, to die like that. He pictured the water, glistening, how beautiful that must be, before you approach the icy smack. Every bone in your body just breaks. Or maybe you drown; he wasn't sure.

One morning he stood up out of his bed.

He was pretty sure he was going to die.

He took off all his clothes.

He walked down a hallway.

Wasn't sure where he was headed.

He was being put into an ambulance.

When he came to, he was again walking down a hall.

A phone was ringing; he answered it. It was his friend Joanne. She told him his stepmother had bought him a place to live, a shack in the country.

When he'd stayed with his dad and Agnes, he had told them he wanted to live in the country. He had circled listings in the paper for ranches in Kentucky, huge acreages you could buy for basically nothing. Bob argued to Agnes and his dad that he could handle living alone somewhere like that on disability, and apparently they had listened.

He didn't know how Joanne knew that Agnes had bought him a place BUT IT WAS TRUYE:

He drove up there the first time. It was way into the middle of nowhere.

It wasn't much: a trailer, and some sort of shell of a half-built structure connected to it.

Agnes cleaned, or tried to. It was pitiful. Tiny little fridge. Shower he couldn't even stand in.

Before dusk, THE FAMILLY got in their car and drove off.

He crawled into the sleeping bag they'd laid across the floor. He examined the topography of the filth now level with his eyes.

It was all lit up by the moon, which on that particular night was monstrous.

In a few hours, they'd be pulling into their big garage, his dad and Agnes.

They'd be unlocking the door to their big house and getting in their bed.

Maybe they'd rest a little more easily now that he had somewhere to be, that it'd take him longer now if he wanted to show up at their door. Or at least now they had a place to send him back to each time he tried.

The moon bathed him and the filthy floor white.

He thought back to that very first night he was locked in that very first cell in Herrick Hospital. The first time he felt really alone.

That was ten years ago.

Something he thought about was the fact that, in that first cell, and all the others—this crowded decade he had just lived—he had felt alone often but he had never actually been alone. He'd always been surrounded by people—nurses and orderlies and doctors with their pens and judgmental eyes, other people like him who were trying to understand why they'd been thrown in a cell and injected with things. Roommates and bunkmates snoring and breathing, their hair in drains. Fellow bodies too high or drunk or sick to move, fallen sometimes into piles.

He had rarely, if never, actually been alone.

This, this shack in the desert, this was different.

This, lying beneath a big white moon, this was the thing he had always sought, he just hadn't realized it until right now.

He finally had peace.

Bob realized he was NOW IN PARADISE:

And there, for the rest of his life, he would more or less remain.

The Fifth Portrait

The manuscript's final lines were a description of himself.

Of the man he had ultimately become.

And an assessment of how he felt he stacked up in the grand scheme of things.

IM STILL ON MEDS, AS LONG AS THE GOV. PAYS FOR THE SHIT, ILL KEEP TAKING IT: THE WITNESSES AND MORMONS DROP BY A COUPLE TIMES A YEAR AND SAY HOW CLOSE TO THE END OF THE WORLD WE ARE, BUT I TELL THEM IN THE NEW TESTIMENT WHEN THE ARMIES SURROUND JERUSALUM, AND JERUSALUM IS DESTROYED, CHRIST WILL APPEAR IN HEAVEN ON HIS THROWN IN THE GOLDEN KINGDOM: I REALLY AM HOPING FOR THAT DAY, BELEVE IT OR NOT: I HAVE UNLIMITED CALLING ON THE PHONE, AND REALLY DONT KNOW ANYONE TO WELL ANYMORE. I OFYEN WONDER IF ANYONE WIOLL NOTICE IF I DIED, LET ALONE HAVE A FUNERALL: I HAVE TWO FEMAIL DOGS NOW, JENNA AND EBOMNY, WHO I GOT FROM THE NEIGHBORS AND THEIR EXELLENT COIMPANY, BUT KEEP ME FROM GOING ANYWHERE, BUT WHO CARES, IM 55 AND SEEING HOW MOST 55 YEAROLDS ARE DOING IM HAPPY WITH WHAT I GOT: IT MAY NOT MEEN MUCH TO OTHERS BUT SEEING TYTHE SHAPE OF WHAT OTHER 55 YEAROLDS ARE IN I HAVE EVERYTHING AND MORE I EVER WANTED: SATALITE TV, A HOME, A

NEW CAR MY FATHER GOT ME A COUPLE YEARS AGO,
MUSIC EQUIPMENT, AND ACES TO THE INTERNET, AND
UNLIMMITED PHONE CALLING, FOOD, AND TWO DOGS::
THAT'S ENOUGHH, NOIT TO MENTION TOTLE PEACE OF
MIND AND A NINE ACRE RANCH IN THE COUNTRY: I
HAVE TIME FO RSTUFF, AND THAT'S WHAT COUNTS;
I HAVE NEVER BEEN MARRIED, NEVER HAD KID AND
DON'T WANT ANY: THE WORLD IS NUTS AND RIGHT NOW
THATS FINE WITH ME:

PARADISE

I had been sitting and reading Bob's manuscript for a few years before I realized there was something I had gotten fundamentally wrong about it: his book was not haphazard or disorganized, not at all.

If anything, it was meticulous. For example, he had typed a number in the top left-hand corner of each page. There were only two spots where he'd wanted to add information after the fact, addenda labeled 7A and 22B (the latter was a paragraph listing people he had met in hospitals or therapy who had committed suicide).

His move north was described on page 51 of 62. It was at this point that his writing changed significantly. Before, he'd written whole scenes, with characters and dialogue and action, and elaborate descriptions. Now entire years passed in single sentences, if they were mentioned at all, and little of the material was about him. His story instead became the story of other people—things he learned from his telephone and satellite dish, stories of his neighbors and family and events of the day.

IN NINETEEN EIGHTY MT. SAINT HELENS ERUPTED AND JOHN LENNOIN WAS ASSASINATED: MUSIC WAS BEGNNING TO CHANGE FOR THE WORSE:

His closest neighbors, Jerry and Sue, remembered when he moved in. It was a cold winter, they said. He was so drugged he could barely function. The only heat he had was a woodstove, and he didn't know how to light it, so they went over and taught him. Sue later found him outside their place, enthusiastically chopping firewood.

They were then already quasi-retired. They'd previously been foster parents, so they "kind of adopted" Bob. He would come by nearly every day, maybe just for five minutes, and they checked in on him as often as they could. They helped him when he had problems. When he complained that people in town were staring at him, they suggested he get some boots, some country clothes, so he'd fit in a little better. They talked to him about bathing. They told him he should be honest with his rotating cast of public psychiatrists about how the drugs made him feel. They recalled he'd been very candid with them about himself when they first met. Jerry remembered: "I think the way he put it, he said, 'You might as well know I'm nuts.'"

IN EIGHTYONE THEY HAD SENT THE FIRST SPACE SHUTTLE AND REGEAN GOT INAUGERATED AND MY SISTER DEBBIE GRADUATED FROM CAL:

The temperature that first summer got to 122 degrees, so he talked his dad into buying him a swamp cooler. He'd sit beneath it and read his Bible and watch TV. His favorite program, on Sunday nights, featured a preacher named Joel Osteen. He liked how optimistic the guy seemed.

He didn't commit to living up north right away. He went back down to the Bay Area a couple more times, including one stay at La Casa Via, which he wrote was his last time ever at a psychiatric hospital. He'd also come down to see concerts with his cousin Tommy, whom he helped move out to Silicon Valley from Minnesota. Tommy did end up working in computers, like he'd long ago whispered during nights at the lake as a kid.

Bob also briefly tried moving out to Minnesota to live with his cousin Jane. Her husband got him a job at the hotel where he worked; Bob was supposed to do room service. He lasted about three weeks before he returned to his trailer in the desert, and the silence there.

IN EIGHTYTWO HINKLY SHOT THE PRESIDENT AND
WAS CONSIDERED INSANE: ANOTHER COOL BAND WAS
PINK FLOYED;

During those first years up north, he'd occasionally go hang
out with some guys in town. They'd argue about the Bible, do
crank, play cards. He went fishing with one friend and panning
for gold with another. He and a friend went to a Jehovah's Wit-
ness hall, but it wasn't for him. Same with the Mormon temple up there; he went but didn't like it. His Christianity became
more confidently independent: I WAS HAPPY JUST TLKING
ABOUT GOD TO ANYONME WITH AS OPINION: I WAS
A HERMIT: SOMEONE WHO STAYS ALONE BECAUSE OF
RELIGIOSE PURPOSES: THAT WAS ME:

He described the dinner when his dad and Agnes agreed to
build the house. An old man and his kid did the work. Bob sat
nearby and watched. He later got a neighbor's brother to help
him put in the deck. Guy was a drunk but he could build a deck.

He got his dog Shivers. One time she was in heat, and all the
dogs in the neighborhood fought over her. He took her down to
his mom's, where she had her puppies. He later gave them all
away at a grocery store, and he very much regretted not keep-
ing one.

IN EIGHTY SIX THE SOVIETS HAD A NUCLEAR POWER
PLANT MELT DOWN, THE CHALLENGER EXPLODED AND
WE SOLD IRAN ARMS: I TOOK A VACATION WITH THE
FAMMILILY TO MANZANILLO MEXICO.

He started doing things himself on the property. He built a
drip line out front. He planted an orange tree and an oleander
and a willow.

He wrote about various relatives' lives. His sisters and stepsisters married, had kids. I got my one mention: EIGHTY SEVEN
DEBBIE HAD A LITTLE GIRL SHE NAMED SANDRA:

ELVIS HAD DIED IN EIGHTY SEVERN BUT I REALLY
NEVER THOIGHT TO MUCH OF HIM: ALSO IN EIGHTY

EIGHT BUSH WAS ELECTED PRESIDENT: IN EIGHTNINE
the BERLIN WALL COLLAPSED:

More nephews and another niece were born. He wrote about other trips, including the ones to Minnesota that I remember. He wrote about coming down to his dad's for Christmas or Thanksgiving. He described a misunderstanding that happened once on vacation, something that got all blown out of proportion. I DIDNT LIKE FAMILLY GATHERINS AFTER THAT SO STAYED AWAY:

He wrote about his neighbors and their affairs. There was a girl who lived down the road who wanted to get involved with him when he first moved up there, but he figured he better not. He wrote fondly of his neighbors Sue and Jerry. He called Jerry THE GUY WHO PROBEBLY DID MORE FOR ME THAN ANYONE.

They moved away eventually, but he'd still call often, they said. They probably had as much of a relationship with him on the phone as they'd had in person, they explained.

Friends, family, former neighbors, all talked about how he'd call them on the phone. A lot of them lost track of him for a while. They had no idea what had become of him for most of the seventies. Then one day, in the eighties or nineties, he called. Some didn't know how he'd gotten their numbers. Old friends. Extended family. His mom's old neighbor Don, who remembered the chainsaw jobs they did, and was sort of familiar with the one boss who had communicated with them only through the mail.

Some people Bob called every year, some every month, some every day.

Some he mailed cassettes of his music. Some he left long messages on their answering machines.

He'd go through periods when he talked to one relative a lot—cousin Tommy, cousin David, his uncle Rollin, then after Rollin died, his son, Neal. Other than his mom, the person he spent the most time on the phone with was his cousin Jane. Sometimes he'd call her more than once a day.

262

They enjoyed his calls, mostly. He was funny, they said. He was curious. He was always reading something or watching something interesting. Those members of my family who are also Christian enjoyed talking to him about that.

A few admitted they found Bob and his calls annoying. He was too full of himself, too proud, especially when it came to his music.

And sometimes his calls weren't pleasant at all. He'd call angry. He'd call and tell stories that were stuck in cells in hospitals or in the halls of Berkeley High. Some people he called did not like the racism—especially those members of my family whose own spouses, children, and grandchildren aren't white: Jane, for example, whose husband is the man she met in Morocco back in the seventies, plus her kids, and their kids, what she described as her "rainbow family."

When Bob talked that way, she'd tell him to cut it out.

Or else sometimes she'd put down the phone and let him talk, because that was the sense she got, that he just needed to talk.

Most grew tired of hearing the same stories, the same complaints.

A few admitted they finally got caller ID.

He listed the possessions he slowly accumulated and the further improvements he made to his home. He painted its interior on his own. I FIXED THINGS THAT BROKE AND LEARNED HOW TO MANAGE QUITE WELL ON THE INCOM I RECEIVED:

After Shivers died, he got another dog and named him Tye. His dad suggested he get Tye neutered and paid for it. Bob regretted this decision often and wrote that this was part of why he valued his father's opinion less than he used to.

Tye eventually got parvo and battled it for a year before it killed him. Bob watched Tye have epileptic fits all night, and then he had to have him euthanized. It was the most depressed he'd ever been in his life.

His trees out front, his orange and willow and oleander,

weathered the summers, the infernal endless heat, and also the cold desert winters. In the spring, they bloomed.

He covered the nineties in less than a page.

In 2000, a new doctor noticed that Bob's medications were making him go blind—he now had to wear thick glasses—and were also wrecking his kidneys and liver. This doctor changed his prescription, and IN THREE WEEKS I STARTED FEELING MORE LIKE A PERSON AND STARTING TO THINK LIKE A HUMAN BEING, AND TALKING: I HAD BARELY ANYTHING TO STAY FOR THE LAST TWENTY YEARS AND NOW WAS COMING OUT OF IT.

My guess, by the way, is that he typed in all capital letters because they were easier for him to see.

Visitors were rare in the new century. His uncle Rollin came to see him in 2001 and then passed away not too long after. Rollin happened to be there the morning his dad called, told Bob to turn on the news. In New York, two planes had flown into the World Trade Center.

Bob thought back to the guy he'd met at the hospital and how Bob predicted that might happen.

THE WAR HAD BEGUN, Bob wrote, by which he meant the one between Christians and Muslims. He discussed his understanding of Islam, which he'd studied, and the things it shared with his own religion. He added that he'd liked that guy at the hospital, as well as the family from Iran whom he'd met at another hospital, the ones who had just been rescued on a top-secret mission.

WAR LEADS TO EVERYTHING WRONG

He talked about how terrible health care had gotten. How every time he went in there he had some new doctor and he could say or get away with whatever he wanted. He talked about how ridiculous it was, that whatever he said determined his sanity.

Only his cousin Jane seemed to remember him talking about writing his manuscript and his decision to send it to me. He worked very hard on it, by her recollection. "He was afraid that people would believe that everything he said wasn't true," she said.

He finished it sometime after he voted for Barack Obama, in November 2008, which he mentioned toward the end. He mailed it to me the following fall.

When I first started trying to write something about Bob, I didn't tell him what I was doing. It was just a piece of writing for a class; I had no intention of publishing any of it.

I would have rather been honest with him right away, but I knew he talked on the phone with his mom a lot, and I worried he'd mention it to her, and soon enough word would get back to Agnes and Gene or someone, and they'd ask questions I didn't yet have answers to, like what I was writing, or what I planned to do with it, or whether I was going to favor the right side of the divorce or the wrong one.

In other words, I guessed (accurately, as it turned out) some people might be quite upset by the idea of a piece of writing based on something Bob had begun.

On the rare occasion when I did talk to Bob on the phone in the years that followed, I was careful to avoid the topics of his writing and mine as much as I could. Sometimes I'd feel him wanting to bring these topics up, and I wouldn't let him. I'd stick my paddle in the water and steer our canoe another way.

I did go see him again, though, a year or two after he mailed the manuscript to me.

I was back home and talked my little brother into driving up there with me. I said he should visit our uncle once in his life. It was a frigid December day, pouring rain, our windshield wipers thumping and semis roaring past.

This visit was much like my first, five years before. Bob

greeted us outside, and as we walked in, he popped a VHS tape into a player.

A still image of a mountain appeared on his TV screen. Then another. It was a slide show. Photos, I realized, of the hiking trip with the donkeys and Piute, back in 1969.

My brother and I sat on his sofa. Bob stood there, his jaw slack, looking at them. Pale browns and scraggly greens. Alpine lakes like blue diamonds. Alien white glaciers.

He looked at me, said, "Ain't that something, man?"

I told him yeah, that was something.

He sat in his chair and lit a cigarette.

There was a bowl of pills on his kitchen table, a constellation of little orange bottles beside it.

He gestured toward his books, which had grown more numerous and been organized, it seemed, since my last visit. There were several squat shelves of them, and other smaller shelves affixed to the walls.

"Here are my Bibles," he said, pointing to a cluster. "Here are my history books," pointing at another, and "Here are my books about war."

There were knives on the walls, too, in display cases. Beneath them were placards he'd typed, explaining things about each of them.

I remarked to Bob that it was funny how presentational it all seemed, "given that you're a hermit."

He nodded. "It's so people know about me when I die," he said, and laughed like he wanted me to laugh, too, so I did.

In around 2013 Bob must have gotten email, or at least my email address, because his messages would now appear in my inbox every so often. Some were short, some were long. He gave his opinions about Hitler and Darwin and encouraged me to watch the show *Ancient Aliens*. Into the next year, he emailed me opinions about politics (he particularly loathed John Boehner) and stories about how, when he was a teenager, he was given pills that made him allergic to the sun. He also sent an envelope that contained a mood ring and a pen in the shape of a guitar. In an accompanying letter, he explained that he'd written a thirty-seven-page philosophical treatise entitled "When We Were Monkeys." He explained he'd written it kind of like Joan of Arc, just listening directly to God.

It weighed on me that I hadn't gone to visit him again, to speak openly about the potential of collaborating on his project. I vaguely planned to go at the end of the year—Christmas 2014—when I'd have some money saved and time off from my job. I imagined bringing him a copy of what I had written to that point, and talking with him about why I'd done things the way I had. I'd let him think about it for as long as he needed, and we would proceed only if he wanted to. I'd let him tell me all the ways in which I'd gotten his story wrong, of course, and fix them. I'd apologize for not being honest sooner. I'd finally apologize for breaking his step. If he was into it, together we'd approach the problem of how to tell his mom and dad and Agnes and everyone else about what we intended to do.

He emailed me on my birthday, in June.

"HAPPY BIRTHDAY;;;I cant believe your twenty seven;;;THATS THE AGE I RETIRED AT!!!!!!!!!!jimi hendrix died at that age;;;;;;anyways;;hope alls well;;;;;"

That one I responded to, saying: "Thank you!"

That July, the summer Bob was sixty, my aunt Heather rather arbitrarily decided to visit her brother. She'd been up there only a few times in the last thirty years. One day something struck her, she said, and she decided to drive north.

She spent several days cleaning, sweating like mad, his two dogs following her around. Years of cobwebs. Years of mouse poop. He sat and watched TV. The blinds in the kitchen hadn't been opened in so many decades they were sealed shut with grime.

He told her late one afternoon that he wanted to go to Red

Lobster. It was like 110 outside, but she said okay. He ordered a ton of food and ate it all with gusto.

Afterward, they sat on his porch laughing. They remembered good times. Summers at Lake L'Homme Dieu.

They hadn't laughed like that in years.

He tried calling her a couple of Sundays later, but for whatever reason, she didn't answer. He tried calling one of his cousins that day, but the cousin didn't answer, either. He also tried calling his mom, but she must have been out, and he didn't leave a message like usual.

Marilyn didn't notice she might have missed a call until the next day, and by the time she called him back, he didn't answer.

"I wonder what he wanted to say," she's said to me many times since. "I wonder what he wanted to *say*."

By Tuesday, dread occupied her.

By Wednesday, it calcified, and she had her niece Jane call him.

He still didn't answer.

She had a friend come over and sit with her as she made the next calls. She and her friend prayed to God, asking Him to take care of Bobby, wherever he was.

She reached a neighbor of his and begged him to go over and check on Bob. She told him to not break in, though, because she didn't want to get in trouble with her ex-husband or his wife, who owned that house.

The neighbor called her back a while later and said he'd gotten inside, that the dogs were in there, barking. They had no food or water, and it was really hot. He said they were going to get a search party together, and they called the sheriff.

It was the sheriff who found him.

He was by his bed.

He wasn't wearing his glasses.

He was naked.

He was kneeling, the sheriff said, as if in prayer.

Or at least that's how Marilyn told it to me. That's what she says she likes to believe.

And so Marilyn and Heather, and Gene and Agnes, gathered in Bob's smoky tomb that hot August Friday. They sorted and threw out most of his possessions.

They went to the coroner. When he asked what Bob's profession had been, Heather blurted out "musician," and that's what is listed on his death certificate, with the "industry" as "music," and "years in occupation" as "40."

The decision was made not to have an autopsy. His causes of death were officially "cardiac dysrhythmia" and "acute myocardial infarction" and "coronary artery disease." Under "other significant conditions contributing to death but not resulting in the underlying cause" is listed only "type II diabetes." The word "schizophrenia," the concept of mental illness generally, his lifelong consumption of psychiatric medications, all got no mention.

I later asked Gene why they didn't get an autopsy, and he said he didn't know what more they could have found out.

Cremation paperwork was signed.

The decision was made not to have a funeral.

They figured out which neighbors could take his dogs. His house was quickly sold. A young couple with kids moved in, a neighbor told me. One of his dogs had to be put down soon after. The neighbor said only Bob could handle her.

Marilyn regretted that she hadn't gotten more days in his home. She wondered often what important things they'd missed. "That was very hard," she said, "being there without Bobby, with all his things."

I asked her what it was like to be with her ex-husband after all these years. "He said we should stay in touch." She laughed. "Isn't that cuckoo?"

That they hadn't had a funeral for her brother really bothered my aunt Heather all that fall and winter.

The next spring, she flew out to Minnesota with his ashes.

She drove up to the lake where I used to go as a kid. Some of his cousins—from both sides of the family—joined her.

They played a CD of some of his songs.

They sprinkled him on the water.

Night fell and the loons wailed.

Or at least I like to think, anyway.

Heather felt it was fortunate she had been to see her brother so recently, because he'd shown her where his writings were. She was able to salvage them and later mailed them to me.

All of his writings arrived one day in the mail, the smoky stack of them.

There were a few short stories and a few handwritten pages about "energy grids." There was the philosophical treatise, which I don't much understand (yet). There was a very entertaining, loosely autobiographical screenplay called BIG DADIO, about a biker who has a `hard time coping with reality`.

A few typewritten pages resembled journal entries. In one dated APRIL 27TH;;2012, he described how he and his doctor had attempted to get his hospital records and determined that THERE IS NO PROOF ANYWHERE THAT I EVER HAD A MENTLE ILLNESS, THE PHYICIATRIC RECORDS ARE GOON: I CAN BUY A GUN NOW:

There were a few pages that resembled poems, some that had clearly spent time on his walls. They're titled things like NOW and THE QUESTION IS and THE SEX LIFE OF A HERMIT. Another is called SORROW. Another REPUTATIONS. Another THE AUTHER, about himself.

A page titled BOBS JOKES; featured a single joke:

WHAT DID THE SCHITZOID SAY AT THE FOOTBALL GAME WHEN

HE SAW THE TEAM HUDDLING ON THE FIELD?

There was also a photocopy of the original manuscript he'd mailed me; I'd been wrong in guessing he hadn't kept one. It turned out, too, that I wasn't the only relative who received this story in the mail. Other relatives, who'd gotten photocopies, threw the pages out. As best as I can tell, they did so because it seemed like he'd written a bunch of lies that would hurt my grandfather.

I didn't know whether I would regret doing this, but I eventually made a time line across my wall, comparing Bob's facts with what I could confirm elsewhere, in letters, report cards, résumés, and the accounts that people were giving me. Sometimes I searched for someone I suspected was a fiction. Sometimes that fiction answered the phone.

His welding certificate. His honorable discharge certificate from the air force, signed January 7, 1980. Dated photographs, too: him and Helen, their arms around each other, their faces like two grinning moons. I found a photo of him and a man seated beside each other on Marilyn's couch; they've got a map spread across both their knees. It was taken right around the time when Bob wrote that he and Wess drove to Louisiana. Nobody I showed the photo to recognized the man, however, nor did they remember anyone named Wess.

I found another photo of Bob walking with his back to the camera in front of his mom's house beside his little black dog Wendy. I had long wondered whether this dog was real; he stopped mentioning her in the manuscript but also didn't say what had become of her. The photo had long sat on my desk, but I hadn't noticed her in a shadow by his side. It was as if she had somehow appeared there.

But Gene remembered her, remembered she was a good dog, and that Merna, the older lady who cooked and cleaned for them, gave her to Bob. Marilyn vaguely remembered having to go to a school in Marin because something had happened; perhaps someone had put that dog in a dryer.

Many people disagreed with Bob's recollection of one thing or another, of course. There remain many people I tried to find but couldn't, like everyone he knew in the hospitals, and many others I tried to reach and never heard back from, like Kenny Rogers.

That said, things really seemed to line up, in terms of where he said he was, and when, and what else would have been going on in the world.

The only historical events he described that didn't seem to fit felt relatively small: I don't believe there was a gas crisis the year he worked at the ARCO station in Walnut Creek, though there had been one back in 1973. Also, the seven-headed snake that Patty Hearst had posed in front of wasn't painted on a wall but on a sheet and she wasn't held in Piedmont. And while the SLA didn't have a theme song of their own, they did sort of adopt the B. B. King song "Better Not Look Down."

The only detail from Bob's life that no one I spoke to found familiar was not the one I would have predicted: nobody recalled him getting in a car accident when he was in the band with the veterans.

Often I'd tell people a story, and they'd laugh because they hadn't thought of that for forty years, man. Often people would marvel at the tiny details he had right—the price, brand names, the makes and models of cars. I learned that Dorothy who ran the halfway house had passed away, as had her neighbor Richard. But his ex-wife, Jenny, did remember my uncle: "He was kind of a short, sturdy guy and he had really pretty blue eyes." She couldn't be too sure, but most everything he recalled about the time he spent with them at the property called "Gambetta" sounded like it could be right to her. (That had been the surname of the Italians who'd homesteaded there before.) She said it was so bizarre I was calling because that whole property had just burned in a big wildfire. Her only memory of my uncle was that he had a chicken, a hen, that he'd hold in his arms and hypnotize.

The man Bob called "Piute"—which was also a nickname; he was not actually "an Indian"—also said everything my uncle remembered about their summers hiking together sounded right to him, other than the part about saving Bob's life from a den of scorpions. He was there both years Bob was. More than anyone else I spoke with, Piute was very curious about why I'd tracked him down, what had become of Bob. "Did Bob become famous?" he asked.

Even my mom, who always said her memory was bad, squinted when I asked about a motel they stayed at on a drive back from Minnesota, and about how she lost a stuffed bunny (nobody else had remembered this). "I did have a bunny," she said. "She had a little apron."

Another time, when I asked her about a neighbor at Lake L'Homme Dieu, an old pirate guy who perhaps lived with "two girlfriends," she nodded that there were two old women around, maybe his sisters, and he did kind of seem like a pirate. She said his name would have been spelled "Perry."

"Oh, I've got Mr. Perry's seashells!" she exclaimed.

We were standing in my childhood home; she walked a few feet to a cupboard. She removed a great glass antique mayonnaise jar and held it out to me. Inside were hundreds of tiny shells, pink and white and yellow, even a tiny ancient sea horse.

How she ended up with them, she couldn't recall.

It took some doing, but I did find her, the girl he had always wondered about.

"That was my stepfather's name, Triantopolous," she said. She hadn't heard that name in a long time.

She had gone to the same school as Bob but didn't remember him, and certainly didn't remember ever going to his house. She must have been in a different class, like he'd said. She talked about all that she was going through back then, how hard it was. "At that time, I probably wouldn't have noticed something as innocuous as a kid who had a crush on me but was afraid to talk to me," she explained.

Bob had wondered whether she'd moved, so I asked her if she had.

"Yes," she said, "we moved to Europe."

She said she was sorry about my uncle.

"I'm glad you're real," I said.

His cousin Jane, who'd spent so much time with him on the phone, wasn't surprised in the least that his manuscript seemed to be remarkably accurate. Bob had an "excellent memory," she said.

She remembered how, back when she'd moved out to Berkeley to live with her aunt and have her baby, Bob had just gotten a job as a logger. First time he got a paycheck, she remembered, he went out and spent it on a dress for her newborn.

He was an "important person," she said. "He told me you were going to write his book," she went on.

I reminded her that couldn't be true.

She sounded unbothered by my objection. She said he had always seemed "comfortable and confident" that I was going to "get the story out there."

When my aunt Heather mailed me her brother's writings, she sent some other things she thought I'd like from his home. They arrived in a giant yellow tube.

First was another pen in the shape of a guitar.

Then there was a poster, about two feet by three, an enlargement of a photograph of the two of us taken at the lake in Minnesota when I was little. She said it had hung on the wall near his bathroom. I don't remember seeing it either time I went to his house, though sometimes I think maybe I did see it the second time I visited him, saw it and tried not to. There was so much I was sorting out back then. There is, of course, a lot I haven't still. A lot, I'm sure, I never will.

In the photo, we're in the back of a speedboat. I look about four or five. I'm wearing an enormous orange life preserver and sunglasses and a baseball cap. I'm looking just to the side, at the water rushing under us, and I look, for a child especially, quite serious. It's a beautiful shot, our heads stacked one atop the other, perfectly centered.

My uncle is behind me, his face obscured by his cap.

He's half-smiling.

And while it's hard to see his eyes, he seems to be looking right into the lens.

Acknowledgments

A Kind of Mirraculas Paradise owes its existence to my incredible agent, Chris Parris-Lamb, and my publisher at Scribner, Nan Graham. Thank you both for believing in this book. I'm forever indebted to my brilliant and indefatigable editors, Kathryn Belden and Daniel Loedel. Thank you to everyone who worked on the project at both the Gernert Company and Simon & Schuster. Thank you to Kate Lloyd. Thank you to Nick Greene, who knows what he did.

Grateful to those I hired to help with the book: Publicist Kathy Daneman; my wonderful assistant, Alex Cornacchia; my brother-in-law, Andy Dubbin, for designing the *AKOMP* website; fact checkers Jane C. Hu and Sarah Edwards, whose thoroughness I will forever appreciate; Natalie Villacorta, who provided invaluable interview transcription.

Thank you, Dale Eisinger, for digitizing Uncle Bob's music, as featured at the beginning of the audiobook. Thank you to Mike Noble of Simon & Schuster Audio for including it and for the team's work on the audiobook. Shout-out to actor Pete Simonelli, who was a great Bob.

Huge thanks to Chris Ritter, who drew the gorgeous hardcover tour announcement artwork and who went on the road with me, who helped me dress and pack my bags. Thanks to the amazing writers who joined me in conversation during the hardcover launch: Meredith Talusan, Esmé Weijun Wang, Anita Badejo, Amanda Chicago Lewis, Lucas Mann, Matthew Spellberg, Elmo Keep, Adrian Nicole LeBlanc, Jessica Hopper, and Anne Helen Petersen.

Thank you to the Bethlem Museum of the Mind for letting us use William Kurelek's *Out of the Maze* on the cover of the paperback edition. I saw this painting in person in early 2016 and it gutted me. I encourage anyone who can to go see the painting in person.

Through the years I worked on this project, so many people have read, spoken with me about relevant topics, or otherwise assisted, in ways big and small. Extra special thanks to draft readers/interlocutors: Rob Moor, Matthew Spellberg, Will Guzzardi, Drew Philp, Andre Perry, Chelsea Cox, Blair Braverman, Ellen Daly, Quince Mountain, Eliana Parnas, Amanda Shapiro, Nicolás Medina Mora, Anita Badejo, Soth "Cupcake" Owens, Jeff Dubbin, Bob Plantenberg, Amanda Chicago Lewis, Ron Schraiber, John Rozehnal, Andrew Rozehnal, Amy Philp, Elmo Keep, Julia Furlan, Heben Nigatu, Vinny Eng, Nichole Perkins, Jaquira Díaz, and Meredith Talusan. Shout-out to all the Slackers. Thank you to Jeff Sharlet, and to the MacDowell Colony, where I finally figured out how to finish it.

Thanks to the professors who worked with me on embryonic versions of the project and who generally taught me how to write, especially my thesis directors at Brown and Iowa respectively, Doug Brown and David Hamilton. Thank you, Catherine Imbriglio. Thank you, Augusto Andres. Thank you, David Vogelstein, for teaching me to leave blood on the courtroom floor.

Much gratitude to my therapist, A.

Much love to all my friends and family, blood and chosen. Thank you, Jeff and Karen. Thank you, Jane. Thank you, Grandmo. Thank you, Mom.

Hugest conceivable thanks to my husband Rob Dubbin for all the ways you supported me and ensured this book made it to planet earth. Love you the most. Honk.

Thank you to my cats, who don't know I've written a book, and would not care if they did.

Thank you, Uncle Bob. Sorry about your step. I agree the world is nuts.